INTERNET ADDRESS BOOK WITH COMPUTER DATA FILES

Professional Version

Title Page

"**Internet Address Book With Computer Data Files - Professional Version**"
Printed in the United States of America.
Published by James Russell Publishing
780 Diogenes Drive, Reno, NV 89512
SAN # 295-852X

"**Internet Address Book With Computer Data Files - Professional Version**"
Written by James Russell © July 2000
Illustrations by James Russell
First Printed Edition © July 2000
ISBN No. 0-916367-12-6
Electronic Edition July 2000 (No ISBN Change)

This book can be purchased from:

Any major bookstore via special order. You may order direct from the following:

- Amazon.com
- Barnes & Noble
- Borders Books
- Walden Books
- Books-A-Million
- Chapters.ca (Canada)
- Varsity Books.com (College Bookstores)
- Your local bookstore.
- Visit our Website: http://www.powernet.net/~scrnplay for free trapshooting lessons and where to find professionals who give lessons (some are listed in this book).

DEDICATED TO

The Lord shall rescue from the pit of despair lifting thee to a high place.

SCRIPTURE

I rescued the poor who cried for help,
and the fatherless who had none to assist him — Job 9:12

IN MEMORY OF

My Loving Mother and Father.

BEST WISHES

To You!

TABLE OF CONTENTS

"The Book Every Computer Owner Must Have!"

Log Your Data — Prevent Disaster!

SIX REASONS WHY YOU NEED THIS BOOK

1. COMPUTER FAILURE

You lose everything when memory conflicts and software crashes, even the file data itself can become corrupted and a backup will *not* work (see *Backing Up Your Data*). You lose *all* if your hard disk drive fails! Settings and passwords are gone forever. This book helps you to restore your data, fast!

2. HARDWARE SETTINGS

When hardware fails, you now have a record of the settings used and a handy guide to contact the manufacturer for resolution. All critical data and settings are logged.

3. INSURANCE RECORD

Fire, theft, hard disk crash, virus attack, CMOS & BIOS errors will destroy all data. Insurance may pay if you have proper records. You'll have them with this book!

4. SOFTWARE LOG

Log your personal settings to make it easy to reset them when you have to reinstall a software program. Record installation settings to make the job easy!

5. INTERNET ADDRESSES

Log your favorite Websites with user names, pass words, ID numbers, etc. If your Internet browser bookmarks fail, you still have them all - nothing beats a hard copy!

6. BE SAFE - PROTECT YOUR DATA!

You'll be glad you purchased this book when data loss occurs!

WHY THE BOOK WAS WRITTEN

Data is critical and to lose it is disaster. Conflicts in computer systems, memory and software is much too frequent and when it comes time to restore the lost data and settings, it can be a nightmare of major proportions: digging up each password, serial number, key number, and that's just to reinstall programs! Then you scream when you discover you forgot the little unique procedures and settings that must be made during installation to make the program run properly. The solution? This book! It's all logged down on paper and cannot be corrupted. Nothing beats a hard copy as you well know by now; computers can't be trusted!

Surfing the Internet, visiting sites, forgetting passwords or other access codes assigned to you is absolutely frustrating. Now you can simply flip the pages of this book and find them with ease. What to do when your Web browser bookmarks or computer fails? You'll have a complete accurate record to easily locate and restore all of your contacts and system data! No more searching through user manuals, flipping over devices to find serial numbers, etc. When you need information on your software or hardware, it's all logged here for quick reference!

REMEMBER WHEN YOU LOST A PASSWORD?

What a pain it can be trying to memorize all the different passwords assigned to you! It's easy to forget. Sure, you can e-mail the Web site for the password, but you have to wait– sometimes days—just to get it. Use this book to enter you username and password for each Web site and it's just a flip of the page away. No interruption in your workflow.

LOSING ALL YOUR FAVORITE INTERNET WEB SITE BOOKMARKS

Suddenly your browser locks up and you discover you can no longer access your favorite Internet Web sites. A software or memory failure corrupted the file and all of your bookmarks are lost, permanently! Listing your favorite Web sites in this book will allow you to reinstall the bookmarks into your computer with ease. No lost data!

THE DAY YOUR COMPUTER BIOS BATTERY DIED

The BIOS battery will fail, it is 100% guaranteed that it will! When it does, say goodbye to all your setup file data. Your computer will not start up automatically. Most people have to take the computer in for repair and these repairs are not cheap. There are firms that will charge over $100 just to replace the battery and reset the setup data files. Plus, you'll have to wait days, even a week or more, just to get your computer out of the shop. With this book, you can open the case of your computer, pop in a battery, insert your setup file data and be back in business in fifteen minutes.

VIRUS ATTACK

You should have antivirus software installed on your computer; however, the software will kill the virus, but may not restore any setting in your setup program (CMOS & BIOS). Without these settings the computer will not run. This book will allow you to log in all your setup settings so you can quickly get back to work.

ABOUT THIS BOOK

FEATURES

- Supports *fifty* Web sites with full contact postal mail address, e-mail, URL, multiple contact names, phone & fax, key words, links, search criteria, etc. *Twenty-seven* entries per Web site listing.
- A highly comprehensive listing no other Internet address book has!
- Supports log entries for *six* computers. More than enough for any home or small business!
- Supports *eight* devices per computer a total of *forty-eight* devices. Not many people have eight devices on a computer, but just in case — it's all here!
- Valuable back up advice to prevent data loss.
- Supports 22 software programs. You don't need this for games. Use the log files for critical programs; word processing, illustration, financial files, etc. Few businesses use more than 15 critical programs, but we included more, just in case.

  - ✓ Primarily, this book is a handy address book to maintain Internet addresses and contact records. If you have ever tried to use a typical address book you found it totally inadequate for Internet use. This book is 100% designed for Web surfers and professionals to maintain Internet contacts.
  - ✓ As an additional feature the book allows you to log in all the data you need to prevent disaster from computer failure, fire, flood, theft resulting in loss of your data!
  - ✓ You can record Web sites that link to your site.
  - ✓ You'll record Websites that sell your product.
  - ✓ No confusion. Before you send an e-mail check your log entry to remind you of who, what, when, where, how and why you are sending the message. Your e-mail messages will be precise and to the point.
  - ✓ The book permits you to log in critical computer device settings. If one of the settings is accidentally switched you can quickly fix the problem!
  - ✓ Once you try the *Internet Address Book — Professional Version* you'll appreciate just how valuable it is.

Don't Wait Until You Lose Your Data — Use This Book Now!

BACKING UP YOUR DATA - THE RIGHT WAY TO DO IT!

Many people learn the hard way and it is right painfully hard to accept the diagnosis from the computer repair man "Your data is destroyed." The confused customer replies "How can this be? I made a backup?" The computer doctor sighs "Your back up disks cannot be recognized by the backup program. The files are there, but unrecoverable."

What happened? The customer used a dedicated backup program, but when the computer's hard drive crashed it could no longer recognize the back up disks, even reinstalling the backup program on the new hard disk, the drive would not recognize the backup disk! Lesson to be learned? Don't buy a backup program. Don't even use the backup program that comes with your computer!

We learned the hard way and lost an entire book that took us over three years to design, write and format. We don't trust backup programs anymore – and we have never lost data since!

1. Save your money and data by not using any computer backup program.
2. Never compress your backup data. Just copy the files as is. Compression can fail!
3. For Windows users use Windows Explorer and copy the files to your backup disk.
4. Back up frequently. Just ask yourself if you can afford to lose the data you have today.
5. Take advantage of free disk backup space on the Internet.
6. Keep your backup disk out of your home so thieves, fire or flood can't destroy your disk.
7. Do not rely on your software's built-in back up command — it may fail. Back up the entire program. This way you'll also save your unique preference settings, macros, etc., along with your data files.
8. You can just back up your data files, but to preserve all the preferences you have set within your software program, back up the entire program with the data files. You should have at least one such back up. This way you don't have to reinstall the program, just copy it back onto the hard disk and in minutes you are back in business.
9. Make another copy of your backup disk. Place it where nobody else knows where it is. Remember, your back up disk can be stolen, damaged or accidentally thrown away. It's a good idea to have an extra back up where only *you* know where it is.
10. Be dedicated in backing up your data often. It is a very painful and expensive experience to lose all of your hard work, time and labor. Back up now! Invest in a quality rewritable disk drive for your backup media.

INSTRUCTIONS FOR USING THE WEBSITE LOG

Below is an example to follow. Notice this Web site log contains all the information you will need to contact the Internet firm by postal mail, phone, e-mail and obtain access to the site using your ID number, password, username, etc. If your Internet browser's bookmark file fails? No problem... it's all here! Use the log for all of your daily contacts. Use the space to the right of the page to insert additional notations.

EXAMPLE - WEBSITE LOG A

Web Site Name: Great Books, Trapshooting etc. **NOTES**
Company Name: James Russell Publishing
Contact Person 1: James Russell
Contact Person 2: Jennifer Saunders
Purchase Order # 214790 **Invoice #** 786
Date: January 15, 2000
Title 1: Publisher **Dept.** Administration
Title 2: Distributor Rep. **Dept.** Sales
Address: 780 Diogenes Drive
City: Reno
State: Nevada **Zip:** 89512
Country: USA **County:** Washoe
Phone 1: 775-348-8711 **Ext:** 411
Phone 2: 775-348-8711 **Ext:** 339
Fax 1: 775-348-8711
Fax 2: 775-348-8711
Email: scrnplay@powernet.net
URL: www.powernet.net/~scrnplay
User Name: BestBooks **CS=Case Sensitive**:Yes
User ID: 4779132 **Reminder:** Good books
Password: 897Books1 **Confirm #** Cu47 **CS:** Yes
Link to: Book Retail Web Sites, Writing, Sports
Search Word: address book, trap shooting secrets
Listed On: Excite, Amazon.com, Barnes&Noble
Catagory: Computers, Entertainment, Sports
Product: Books, Popcrackers, Screenwriting
Also See: Bookstores & www.bakertaylor.com
Notes: Ask JR Publishing to link to our web site.
Order three copies of this internet book for gifts.

NOTES:

WEB SITE LOG ____

NOTES

Web Site Name:______________________
Company Name:______________________
Contact Person 1:______________________
Contact Person 2:______________________
Purchase Order #:________**Invoice #:**_______
Date:__________________
Title 1:________________**Dept:**__________
Title 2:________________**Dept:**__________
Address:______________________________
City:________________________________
State:________________**Zip:**__________
Country:____________**County:**__________
Phone 1:____________________**Ext:** _____
Phone 2:____________________**Ext:** _____
Fax 1:______________________________
Fax 2:______________________________
Email:______________________________
URL:________________________________
User Name:________________**CS:** _______
User ID: ______________**Reminder:**_________
Password:_________**Confirm #:**_____**CS:**____
Search Word:___________________________
Listed On:_____________________________
Catagory:______________________________
Product:_______________________________
Also See:______________________________
Notes:________________________________
____
_______________________________________.

NOTES:

____
____
____
____
____
____
____
____
____
____
____
____.

WEB SITE LOG _____

NOTES

Web Site Name:________________________
Company Name:________________________
Contact Person 1:______________________
Contact Person 2:______________________
Purchase Order #:________**Invoice #:**_______
Date:___________________
Title 1:_______________**Dept:**__________
Title 2:_______________**Dept:**__________
Address:______________________________
City:________________________________
State:_________________**Zip:**__________
Country:____________**County:**__________
Phone 1:___________________**Ext:** ______
Phone 2:___________________**Ext:** ______
Fax 1:_______________________________
Fax 2:_______________________________
Email:_______________________________
URL:________________________________
User Name:________________**CS:** _______
User ID: ______________**Reminder:**_________
Password:__________**Confirm #:**_____**CS:**____
Search Word:___________________________
Listed On:____________________________
Catagory:_____________________________
Product:______________________________
Also See:_____________________________
Notes:_______________________________
____
____.

NOTES:

____
____
____
____
____
____
____
____
____
____
____
____.

WEB SITE LOG ____

NOTES

Web Site Name:__________________________
Company Name:__________________________
Contact Person 1:________________________
Contact Person 2:________________________
Purchase Order #:_________**Invoice #:**_______
Date:____________________
Title 1:________________**Dept:**___________
Title 2:________________**Dept:**___________
Address:________________________________
City:___________________________________
State:__________________**Zip:**___________
Country:_____________**County:**___________
Phone 1:_____________________**Ext:** ______
Phone 2:_____________________**Ext:** ______
Fax 1:_________________________________
Fax 2:_________________________________
Email:__________________________________
URL:___________________________________
User Name:________________**CS:** _______
User ID: ______________**Reminder:**_________
Password:__________**Confirm #:**_____**CS:**____
Search Word:____________________________
Listed On:______________________________
Catagory:_______________________________
Product:________________________________
Also See:_______________________________
Notes:_________________________________
____
____.

NOTES:

WEB SITE LOG ____

NOTES

Web Site Name:________________________
Company Name:________________________
Contact Person 1:______________________
Contact Person 2:______________________
Purchase Order #:________**Invoice #:**_______
Date:___________________
Title 1:________________**Dept:**__________
Title 2:________________**Dept:**__________
Address:_______________________________
City:_________________________________
State:_________________**Zip:**__________
Country:____________**County:**__________
Phone 1:___________________**Ext:** _____
Phone 2:___________________**Ext:** _____
Fax 1:_______________________________
Fax 2:_______________________________
Email:_______________________________
URL:________________________________
User Name:________________**CS:** ______
User ID: ______________**Reminder:**________
Password:_________**Confirm #:**_____**CS:**____
Search Word:___________________________
Listed On:____________________________
Catagory:____________________________
Product:_____________________________
Also See:____________________________
Notes:_______________________________
____
____.

NOTES:

____
____
____
____
____
____
____
____
____
____
____
____.

WEB SITE LOG ____

NOTES

Web Site Name:__________________________
Company Name:__________________________
Contact Person 1:________________________
Contact Person 2:________________________
Purchase Order #:_________**Invoice #:**_______
Date:____________________
Title 1:________________**Dept:**___________
Title 2:________________**Dept:**___________
Address:________________________________
City:___________________________________
State:__________________**Zip:**___________
Country:_____________**County:**___________
Phone 1:_____________________**Ext:** ______
Phone 2:_____________________**Ext:** ______
Fax 1:_________________________________
Fax 2:_________________________________
Email:__________________________________
URL:___________________________________
User Name:_________________**CS:** _______
User ID: ______________**Reminder:**_________
Password:__________**Confirm #:**_____**CS:**____
Search Word:____________________________
Listed On:______________________________
Catagory:_______________________________
Product:________________________________
Also See:_______________________________
Notes:_________________________________
____
____.

NOTES:

____
____
____
____
____
____
____
____
____
____
____
____.

WEB SITE LOG ____

NOTES

Web Site Name:______________________________
Company Name:______________________________
Contact Person 1:___________________________
Contact Person 2:___________________________
Purchase Order #:________**Invoice #:**_______
Date:____________________
Title 1:________________**Dept:**___________
Title 2:________________**Dept:**___________
Address:_________________________________
City:____________________________________
State:___________________**Zip:**___________
Country:_____________**County:**___________
Phone 1:_____________________**Ext:** ______
Phone 2:_____________________**Ext:** ______
Fax 1:___________________________________
Fax 2:___________________________________
Email:___________________________________
URL:____________________________________
User Name:_________________**CS:** _______
User ID: ______________**Reminder:**________
Password:__________**Confirm #:**_____**CS:**____
Search Word:______________________________
Listed On:________________________________
Catagory:_________________________________
Product:__________________________________
Also See:_________________________________
Notes:____________________________________
____
____.

NOTES:

____
____
____
____
____
____
____
____
____
____
____
____.

WEB SITE LOG ____

NOTES

Web Site Name:___________________________
Company Name:___________________________
Contact Person 1:_________________________
Contact Person 2:_________________________
Purchase Order #:_________**Invoice #:**_______
Date:_____________________
Title 1:_________________**Dept:**___________
Title 2:_________________**Dept:**___________
Address:__________________________________
City:_____________________________________
State:___________________**Zip:**___________
Country:_____________**County:**___________
Phone 1:_____________________**Ext:** ______
Phone 2:_____________________**Ext:** ______
Fax 1:___________________________________
Fax 2:___________________________________
Email:___________________________________
URL:____________________________________
User Name:_________________**CS**: _______
User ID: _______________**Reminder:**_________
Password:__________**Confirm #:**_____**CS**:____
Search Word:_____________________________
Listed On:_______________________________
Catagory:_______________________________
Product:________________________________
Also See:________________________________
Notes:___________________________________
____
____.

NOTES:

____
____
____
____
____
____
____
____
____
____
____
____.

WEB SITE LOG ____

NOTES

Web Site Name:______________________
Company Name:______________________
Contact Person 1:____________________
Contact Person 2:____________________
Purchase Order #:________**Invoice #:**_______
Date:________________
Title 1:______________**Dept:**__________
Title 2:______________**Dept:**__________
Address:_________________________
City:____________________________
State:______________**Zip:**__________
Country:__________**County:**__________
Phone 1:________________**Ext:** ______
Phone 2:________________**Ext:** ______
Fax 1:___________________________
Fax 2:___________________________
Email:___________________________
URL:____________________________
User Name:_____________**CS:** ______
User ID: ____________**Reminder:**_________
Password:_________**Confirm #:**_____**CS:**____
Search Word:_______________________
Listed On:_________________________
Catagory:_________________________
Product:__________________________
Also See:_________________________
Notes:___________________________
____
_____________________________________.

NOTES:

____
____
____
____
____
____
____
____
____
____
____
____.

WEB SITE LOG ____

NOTES

Web Site Name:__________________________
Company Name:__________________________
Contact Person 1:______________________
Contact Person 2:______________________
Purchase Order #:_________**Invoice #:**_______
Date:____________________
Title 1:________________**Dept:**___________
Title 2:________________**Dept:**___________
Address:________________________________
City:__________________________________
State:___________________**Zip:**___________
Country:_____________**County:**___________
Phone 1:____________________**Ext:** ______
Phone 2:____________________**Ext:** ______
Fax 1:_________________________________
Fax 2:_________________________________
Email:_________________________________
URL:__________________________________
User Name:_________________**CS:** _______
User ID: ______________**Reminder:**_________
Password:__________**Confirm #:**_____**CS:**____
Search Word:____________________________
Listed On:______________________________
Catagory:_______________________________
Product:_______________________________
Also See:_______________________________
Notes:_________________________________
____
____.

NOTES:

____
____
____
____
____
____
____
____
____
____
____
____.

WEB SITE LOG ____

NOTES

Web Site Name:_______________________
Company Name:_______________________
Contact Person 1:_____________________
Contact Person 2:_____________________
Purchase Order #:________**Invoice #:**_______
Date:__________________
Title 1:_______________**Dept:**__________
Title 2:_______________**Dept:**__________
Address:____________________________
City:______________________________
State:_________________**Zip:**__________
Country:____________**County:**__________
Phone 1:____________________**Ext:** ______
Phone 2:____________________**Ext:** ______
Fax 1:_____________________________
Fax 2:_____________________________
Email:_____________________________
URL:______________________________
User Name:________________**CS:** _______
User ID: _____________**Reminder:**_________
Password:__________**Confirm #:**_____**CS:**____
Search Word:__________________________
Listed On:___________________________
Catagory:___________________________
Product:____________________________
Also See:____________________________
Notes:______________________________
____
____.

NOTES:
____
____
____
____
____
____
____
____
____
____
____
____.

WEB SITE LOG ____

NOTES

Web Site Name:__________________________
Company Name:__________________________
Contact Person 1:______________________
Contact Person 2:______________________
Purchase Order #:_________**Invoice #:**_______
Date:____________________
Title 1:________________**Dept:**__________
Title 2:________________**Dept:**__________
Address:________________________________
City:____________________________________
State:___________________**Zip:**__________
Country:_____________**County:**__________
Phone 1:_____________________**Ext:** ______
Phone 2:_____________________**Ext:** ______
Fax 1:__________________________________
Fax 2:__________________________________
Email:__________________________________
URL:____________________________________
User Name:_________________**CS:** _______
User ID: ______________**Reminder:**_________
Password:__________**Confirm #:**_____**CS:**____
Search Word:____________________________
Listed On:______________________________
Catagory:_______________________________
Product:________________________________
Also See:_______________________________
Notes:__________________________________
____
____.

NOTES:

____
____
____
____
____
____
____
____
____
____
____
____.

WEB SITE LOG ____

NOTES

Web Site Name:________________________
Company Name:________________________
Contact Person 1:______________________
Contact Person 2:______________________
Purchase Order #:_________**Invoice #:**_______
Date:___________________
Title 1:________________**Dept:**__________
Title 2:________________**Dept:**__________
Address:____________________________
City:______________________________
State:__________________**Zip:**__________
Country:_____________**County:**__________
Phone 1:____________________**Ext:** ______
Phone 2:____________________**Ext:** ______
Fax 1:_____________________________
Fax 2:_____________________________
Email:_____________________________
URL:______________________________
User Name:________________**CS:** _______
User ID: ______________**Reminder:**________
Password:__________**Confirm #:**_____**CS:**____
Search Word:__________________________
Listed On:____________________________
Catagory:____________________________
Product:____________________________
Also See:____________________________
Notes:______________________________
____
_______________________________________.

NOTES:

____
____
____
____
____
____
____
____
____
____
____
____.

WEB SITE LOG ____

NOTES

Web Site Name:________________________
Company Name:________________________
Contact Person 1:______________________
Contact Person 2:______________________
Purchase Order #:________**Invoice #:**_______
Date:____________________
Title 1:________________**Dept:**__________
Title 2:________________**Dept:**__________
Address:______________________________
City:_________________________________
State:__________________**Zip:**__________
Country:_____________**County:**__________
Phone 1:___________________**Ext:** ______
Phone 2:___________________**Ext:** ______
Fax 1:________________________________
Fax 2:________________________________
Email:________________________________
URL:_________________________________
User Name:________________**CS:** _______
User ID: _____________**Reminder:**_________
Password:_________**Confirm #:**_____**CS:**____
Search Word:___________________________
Listed On:____________________________
Catagory:_____________________________
Product:______________________________
Also See:_____________________________
Notes:________________________________
____
____.

NOTES:

____
____
____
____
____
____
____
____
____
____
____
____.

WEB SITE LOG _____

NOTES

Web Site Name:_________________________
Company Name:_________________________
Contact Person 1:_______________________
Contact Person 2:_______________________
Purchase Order #:________**Invoice #:**_______
Date:____________________
Title 1:________________**Dept:**__________
Title 2:________________**Dept:**__________
Address:______________________________
City:________________________________
State:_________________**Zip:**__________
Country:____________**County:**__________
Phone 1:___________________**Ext:** ______
Phone 2:___________________**Ext:** ______
Fax 1:________________________________
Fax 2:________________________________
Email:________________________________
URL:_________________________________
User Name:________________**CS:** _______
User ID: _____________**Reminder:**_________
Password:_________**Confirm #:**_____**CS:**____
Search Word:____________________________
Listed On:______________________________
Catagory:______________________________
Product:_______________________________
Also See:_______________________________
Notes:_________________________________
____
____.

NOTES:

____
____
____
____
____
____
____
____
____
____
____
____.

WEB SITE LOG ____

NOTES

Web Site Name:___________________________
Company Name:___________________________
Contact Person 1:_______________________
Contact Person 2:_______________________
Purchase Order #:_________**Invoice #:**_______
Date:____________________
Title 1:________________**Dept:**___________
Title 2:________________**Dept:**___________
Address:_______________________________
City:__________________________________
State:___________________**Zip:**___________
Country:_____________**County:**___________
Phone 1:_____________________**Ext:** ______
Phone 2:_____________________**Ext:** ______
Fax 1:_________________________________
Fax 2:_________________________________
Email:_________________________________
URL:__________________________________
User Name:_________________**CS:** _______
User ID: _______________**Reminder:**_________
Password:__________**Confirm #:**_____**CS:**____
Search Word:____________________________
Listed On:______________________________
Catagory:_______________________________
Product:________________________________
Also See:_______________________________
Notes:_________________________________
____
____.

NOTES:

____
____
____
____
____
____
____
____
____
____
____
____.

WEB SITE LOG ____

NOTES

Web Site Name:___________________________
Company Name:___________________________
Contact Person 1:_________________________
Contact Person 2:_________________________
Purchase Order #:_________**Invoice #:**_______
Date:____________________
Title 1:________________**Dept:**__________
Title 2:________________**Dept:**__________
Address:_______________________________
City:__________________________________
State:_________________**Zip:**__________
Country:_____________**County:**__________
Phone 1:____________________**Ext:** ______
Phone 2:____________________**Ext:** ______
Fax 1:________________________________
Fax 2:________________________________
Email:_________________________________
URL:__________________________________
User Name:________________**CS:** _______
User ID: ______________**Reminder:**________
Password:__________**Confirm #:**_____**CS:**____
Search Word:____________________________
Listed On:______________________________
Catagory:______________________________
Product:_______________________________
Also See:______________________________
Notes:________________________________
____
____.

NOTES:

____
____
____
____
____
____
____
____
____
____
____
____.

WEB SITE LOG ____

NOTES

Web Site Name:________________________
Company Name:________________________
Contact Person 1:______________________
Contact Person 2:______________________
Purchase Order #:________**Invoice #:**_______
Date:____________________
Title 1:________________**Dept:**__________
Title 2:________________**Dept:**__________
Address:______________________________
City:________________________________
State:________________**Zip:**__________
Country:____________**County:**__________
Phone 1:____________________**Ext:** _____
Phone 2:____________________**Ext:** _____
Fax 1:_______________________________
Fax 2:_______________________________
Email:_______________________________
URL:________________________________
User Name:________________**CS:** ______
User ID: _____________**Reminder:**________
Password:__________**Confirm #:**_____**CS:**____
Search Word:__________________________
Listed On:___________________________
Catagory:____________________________
Product:_____________________________
Also See:____________________________
Notes:______________________________
____
_______________________________________.

NOTES:

____
____
____
____
____
____
____
____
____
____
____
____.

WEB SITE LOG ____

NOTES

Web Site Name:________________________
Company Name:________________________
Contact Person 1:______________________
Contact Person 2:______________________
Purchase Order #:________**Invoice #:**______
Date:____________________
Title 1:________________**Dept:**__________
Title 2:________________**Dept:**__________
Address:______________________________
City:________________________________
State:__________________**Zip:**__________
Country:____________**County:**__________
Phone 1:____________________**Ext:** _____
Phone 2:____________________**Ext:** _____
Fax 1:______________________________
Fax 2:______________________________
Email:_______________________________
URL:________________________________
User Name:________________**CS:** ______
User ID: _____________**Reminder:**________
Password:_________**Confirm #:**_____**CS:**____
Search Word:__________________________
Listed On:___________________________
Catagory:____________________________
Product:_____________________________
Also See:____________________________
Notes:______________________________
____
____.

NOTES:

____
____
____
____
____
____
____
____
____
____
____
____.

WEB SITE LOG ____

NOTES

Web Site Name:__________________________
Company Name:__________________________
Contact Person 1:_______________________
Contact Person 2:_______________________
Purchase Order #:_________**Invoice #:**_______
Date:____________________
Title 1:_________________**Dept:**___________
Title 2:_________________**Dept:**___________
Address:________________________________
City:___________________________________
State:___________________**Zip:**___________
Country:_____________**County:**___________
Phone 1:_____________________**Ext:** ______
Phone 2:_____________________**Ext:** ______
Fax 1:__________________________________
Fax 2:__________________________________
Email:__________________________________
URL:___________________________________
User Name:_________________**CS**: _______
User ID: ______________**Reminder:**_________
Password:__________**Confirm #:**_____**CS**:____
Search Word:____________________________
Listed On:______________________________
Catagory:______________________________
Product:_______________________________
Also See:______________________________
Notes:_________________________________
____
____.

NOTES:

____
____
____
____
____
____
____
____
____
____
____
____.

WEB SITE LOG ____

NOTES

Web Site Name:___________________________
Company Name:___________________________
Contact Person 1:________________________
Contact Person 2:________________________
Purchase Order #:________**Invoice #:**_______
Date:____________________
Title 1:________________**Dept:**__________
Title 2:________________**Dept:**__________
Address:______________________________
City:_________________________________
State:_________________**Zip:**__________
Country:____________**County:**__________
Phone 1:____________________**Ext:** ______
Phone 2:____________________**Ext:** ______
Fax 1:________________________________
Fax 2:________________________________
Email:________________________________
URL:_________________________________
User Name:_______________**CS:** _______
User ID: _____________**Reminder:**________
Password:_________**Confirm #:**_____**CS:**____
Search Word:___________________________
Listed On:_____________________________
Catagory:______________________________
Product:_______________________________
Also See:______________________________
Notes:_________________________________
____
____.

NOTES:

____
____
____
____
____
____
____
____
____
____
____
____.

WEB SITE LOG ____

NOTES

Web Site Name:________________________
Company Name:________________________
Contact Person 1:______________________
Contact Person 2:______________________
Purchase Order #:________**Invoice #:**_______
Date:___________________
Title 1:_______________**Dept:**__________
Title 2:_______________**Dept:**__________
Address:____________________________
City:_______________________________
State:_________________**Zip:**__________
Country:____________**County:**__________
Phone 1:___________________**Ext:** _____
Phone 2:___________________**Ext:** _____
Fax 1:_______________________________
Fax 2:_______________________________
Email:______________________________
URL:_______________________________
User Name:________________**CS:** ______
User ID: _____________**Reminder:**________
Password:_________**Confirm #:**_____**CS:**____
Search Word:__________________________
Listed On:___________________________
Catagory:___________________________
Product:____________________________
Also See:___________________________
Notes:______________________________
____
_______________________________________.

NOTES:

____
____
____
____
____
____
____
____
____
____
____
____.

WEB SITE LOG ____

NOTES

Web Site Name:_______________________
Company Name:_______________________
Contact Person 1:_____________________
Contact Person 2:_____________________
Purchase Order #:_______**Invoice #:**______
Date:_________________
Title 1:______________**Dept:**_________
Title 2:______________**Dept:**_________
Address:___________________________
City:_____________________________
State:_______________**Zip:**_________
Country:___________**County:**_________
Phone 1:__________________**Ext:** _____
Phone 2:__________________**Ext:** _____
Fax 1:____________________________
Fax 2:____________________________
Email:____________________________
URL:_____________________________
User Name:______________**CS:** ______
User ID: _____________**Reminder:**________
Password:_________**Confirm #:**_____**CS:**____
Search Word:_________________________
Listed On:___________________________
Catagory:___________________________
Product:____________________________
Also See:___________________________
Notes:_____________________________
____
_____________________________________.

NOTES:

WEB SITE LOG ____

NOTES

Web Site Name:______________________
Company Name:______________________
Contact Person 1:____________________
Contact Person 2:____________________
Purchase Order #:________**Invoice #:**______
Date:____________________
Title 1:______________**Dept:**__________
Title 2:______________**Dept:**__________
Address:__________________________
City:____________________________
State:_______________**Zip:**__________
Country:____________**County:**__________
Phone 1:__________________**Ext:** _____
Phone 2:__________________**Ext:** _____
Fax 1:____________________________
Fax 2:____________________________
Email:____________________________
URL:_____________________________
User Name:______________**CS:** ______
User ID: ___________**Reminder:**________
Password:_________**Confirm #:**_____**CS:**____
Search Word:_______________________
Listed On:_________________________
Catagory:__________________________
Product:___________________________
Also See:__________________________
Notes:____________________________
____
______________________________________.

NOTES:
____
____
____
____
____
____
____
____
____
____
____
____.

WEB SITE LOG ____

NOTES

Web Site Name:________________________
Company Name:________________________
Contact Person 1:______________________
Contact Person 2:______________________
Purchase Order #:________**Invoice #:**_______
Date:___________________
Title 1:________________**Dept:**__________
Title 2:________________**Dept:**__________
Address:____________________________
City:_______________________________
State:_________________**Zip:**__________
Country:____________**County:**__________
Phone 1:___________________**Ext:** ______
Phone 2:___________________**Ext:** ______
Fax 1:_____________________________
Fax 2:______________________________
Email:______________________________
URL:_______________________________
User Name:______________**CS:** _______
User ID: ______________**Reminder:**________
Password:_________**Confirm #:**_____**CS:**____
Search Word:__________________________
Listed On:___________________________
Catagory:____________________________
Product:____________________________
Also See:____________________________
Notes:______________________________
____
_______________________________________.

NOTES:

____
____
____
____
____
____
____
____
____
____
____
____.

WEB SIRE LOG ____

NOTES

Web Site Name:_______________________
Company Name:_______________________
Contact Person 1:_____________________
Contact Person 2:_____________________
Purchase Order #:________**Invoice #:**_______
Date:___________________
Title 1:________________**Dept:**__________
Title 2:________________**Dept:**__________
Address:_____________________________
City:_______________________________
State:__________________**Zip:**__________
Country:_____________**County:**__________
Phone 1:____________________**Ext:** _____
Phone 2:____________________**Ext:** _____
Fax 1:______________________________
Fax 2:______________________________
Email:______________________________
URL:_______________________________
User Name:________________**CS:** _______
User ID: ______________**Reminder:**_________
Password:__________**Confirm #:**_____**CS:**____
Search Word:__________________________
Listed On:____________________________
Catagory:____________________________
Product:_____________________________
Also See:____________________________
Notes:______________________________
____
_______________________________________.

NOTES:

____
____
____
____
____
____
____
____
____
____
____
____.

WEB SITE LOG ____

NOTES

Web Site Name:___________________________
Company Name:___________________________
Contact Person 1:_________________________
Contact Person 2:_________________________
Purchase Order #:_________**Invoice #:**_______
Date:____________________
Title 1:________________**Dept:**___________
Title 2:________________**Dept:**___________
Address:________________________________
City:___________________________________
State:__________________**Zip:**___________
Country:_____________**County:**___________
Phone 1:_____________________**Ext:** ______
Phone 2:_____________________**Ext:** ______
Fax 1:__________________________________
Fax 2:__________________________________
Email:__________________________________
URL:___________________________________
User Name:_________________**CS:** _______
User ID: ______________**Reminder:**_________
Password:__________**Confirm #:**_____**CS:**____
Search Word:____________________________
Listed On:______________________________
Catagory:_______________________________
Product:________________________________
Also See:_______________________________
Notes:_________________________________
____
____.

NOTES:

____
____
____
____
____
____
____
____
____
____
____
____.

WEB SITE LOG ____

NOTES

Web Site Name:___________________________
Company Name:___________________________
Contact Person 1:________________________
Contact Person 2:________________________
Purchase Order #:_________**Invoice #:**_______
Date:_____________________
Title 1:_________________**Dept:**___________
Title 2:_________________**Dept:**___________
Address:_________________________________
City:____________________________________
State:___________________**Zip:**___________
Country:_____________**County:**___________
Phone 1:______________________**Ext:** ______
Phone 2:______________________**Ext:** ______
Fax 1:___________________________________
Fax 2:___________________________________
Email:___________________________________
URL:____________________________________
User Name:_________________**CS:** _______
User ID: ______________**Reminder:**_________
Password:__________**Confirm #:**_____**CS:**____
Search Word:______________________________
Listed On:________________________________
Catagory:_________________________________
Product:_________________________________
Also See:_________________________________
Notes:___________________________________
____
____.

NOTES:

____
____
____
____
____
____
____
____
____
____
____
____.

WEB SITE LOG _____

NOTES

Web Site Name:__________________________
Company Name:__________________________
Contact Person 1:_______________________
Contact Person 2:_______________________
Purchase Order #:________**Invoice #:**_______
Date:____________________
Title 1:________________**Dept:**___________
Title 2:________________**Dept:**___________
Address:_______________________________
City:__________________________________
State:_________________**Zip:**___________
Country:_____________**County:**___________
Phone 1:____________________**Ext:** ______
Phone 2:____________________**Ext:** ______
Fax 1:_________________________________
Fax 2:_________________________________
Email:_________________________________
URL:__________________________________
User Name:_________________**CS:** _______
User ID: ______________**Reminder:**_________
Password:__________**Confirm #:**_____**CS:**____
Search Word:____________________________
Listed On:______________________________
Catagory:______________________________
Product:_______________________________
Also See:_______________________________
Notes:________________________________
____
____.

NOTES:
____
____
____
____
____
____
____
____
____
____
____
____.

WEB SITE LOG ____

NOTES

Web Site Name:___________________________
Company Name:___________________________
Contact Person 1:________________________
Contact Person 2:________________________
Purchase Order #:_________**Invoice #:**_______
Date:____________________
Title 1:_________________**Dept:**___________
Title 2:_________________**Dept:**___________
Address:_________________________________
City:____________________________________
State:___________________**Zip:**___________
Country:_____________**County:**___________
Phone 1:____________________**Ext:** ______
Phone 2:____________________**Ext:** ______
Fax 1:___________________________________
Fax 2:___________________________________
Email:___________________________________
URL:____________________________________
User Name:_________________**CS:** _______
User ID: _______________**Reminder:**_________
Password:__________**Confirm #:**_____**CS:**____
Search Word:_____________________________
Listed On:_______________________________
Catagory:_______________________________
Product:________________________________
Also See:_______________________________
Notes:__________________________________
____
____.

NOTES:

____
____
____
____
____
____
____
____
____
____
____
____.

WEB SITE LOG ____

NOTES

Web Site Name:_______________________
Company Name:_______________________
Contact Person 1:_____________________
Contact Person 2:_____________________
Purchase Order #:________**Invoice #:**_______
Date:__________________
Title 1:______________**Dept:**__________
Title 2:______________**Dept:**__________
Address:____________________________
City:_______________________________
State:________________**Zip:**__________
Country:____________**County:**__________
Phone 1:___________________**Ext:** ______
Phone 2:___________________**Ext:** ______
Fax 1:_____________________________
Fax 2:_____________________________
Email:_____________________________
URL:______________________________
User Name:_______________**CS:** _______
User ID: _____________**Reminder:**_________
Password:__________**Confirm #:**_____**CS:**____
Search Word:__________________________
Listed On:___________________________
Catagory:___________________________
Product:____________________________
Also See:___________________________
Notes:_____________________________
____
_______________________________________.

NOTES:

____
____
____
____
____
____
____
____
____
____
____
____.

WEB SITE LOG ____

NOTES

Web Site Name:________________________
Company Name:________________________
Contact Person 1:______________________
Contact Person 2:______________________
Purchase Order #:________**Invoice #:**______
Date:__________________
Title 1:_______________**Dept:**__________
Title 2:_______________**Dept:**__________
Address:______________________________
City:_________________________________
State:_________________**Zip:**__________
Country:____________**County:**__________
Phone 1:___________________**Ext:** _____
Phone 2:___________________**Ext:** _____
Fax 1:_______________________________
Fax 2:_______________________________
Email:_______________________________
URL:________________________________
User Name:_______________**CS:** ______
User ID: ______________**Reminder:**________
Password:_________**Confirm #:**_____**CS:**____
Search Word:___________________________
Listed On:____________________________
Catagory:_____________________________
Product:______________________________
Also See:_____________________________
Notes:_______________________________
____
_______________________________________.

NOTES:
____
____
____
____
____
____
____
____
____
____
____
____.

WEB SITE LOG ____

NOTES

Web Site Name:________________________
Company Name:________________________
Contact Person 1:______________________
Contact Person 2:______________________
Purchase Order #:________**Invoice #:**_______
Date:____________________
Title 1:________________**Dept:**__________
Title 2:________________**Dept:**__________
Address:______________________________
City:_________________________________
State:________________**Zip:**__________
Country:____________**County:**__________
Phone 1:____________________**Ext:** ______
Phone 2:____________________**Ext:** ______
Fax 1:_______________________________
Fax 2:_______________________________
Email:_______________________________
URL:_________________________________
User Name:_______________**CS:** _______
User ID: ______________**Reminder:**________
Password:__________**Confirm #:**_____**CS:**____
Search Word:___________________________
Listed On:____________________________
Catagory:_____________________________
Product:______________________________
Also See:_____________________________
Notes:________________________________
____
____.

NOTES:

____
____
____
____
____
____
____
____
____
____
____
____.

WEB SITE LOG ____

NOTES

Web Site Name:__________________________
Company Name:__________________________
Contact Person 1:________________________
Contact Person 2:________________________
Purchase Order #:________**Invoice #:**_______
Date:____________________
Title 1:________________**Dept:**___________
Title 2:________________**Dept:**___________
Address:________________________________
City:___________________________________
State:__________________**Zip:**___________
Country:_____________**County:**___________
Phone 1:____________________**Ext:** ______
Phone 2:____________________**Ext:** ______
Fax 1:__________________________________
Fax 2:__________________________________
Email:__________________________________
URL:___________________________________
User Name:________________**CS:** _______
User ID: _____________**Reminder:**_________
Password:_________**Confirm #:**_____**CS:**____
Search Word:______________________________
Listed On:_____________________________
Catagory:______________________________
Product:_______________________________
Also See:______________________________
Notes:_________________________________
____
____.

NOTES:
____
____
____
____
____
____
____
____
____
____
____
____.

WEB SITE LOG ____

NOTES

Web Site Name:___________________________
Company Name:___________________________
Contact Person 1:_______________________
Contact Person 2:_______________________
Purchase Order #:_________**Invoice #:**_______
Date:____________________
Title 1:________________**Dept:**__________
Title 2:________________**Dept:**__________
Address:________________________________
City:___________________________________
State:__________________**Zip:**___________
Country:_____________**County:**___________
Phone 1:____________________**Ext:** ______
Phone 2:____________________**Ext:** ______
Fax 1:__________________________________
Fax 2:__________________________________
Email:__________________________________
URL:____________________________________
User Name:________________**CS:** _______
User ID: _______________**Reminder:**_________
Password:__________**Confirm #:**_____**CS:**____
Search Word:______________________________
Listed On:______________________________
Catagory:_______________________________
Product:________________________________
Also See:_______________________________
Notes:__________________________________
____
____.

NOTES:

____
____
____
____
____
____
____
____
____
____
____
____.

WEB SITE LOG ____

NOTES

Web Site Name:________________________
Company Name:________________________
Contact Person 1:______________________
Contact Person 2:______________________
Purchase Order #:________**Invoice #:**_______
Date:___________________
Title 1:________________**Dept:**__________
Title 2:________________**Dept:**__________
Address:_____________________________
City:________________________________
State:_________________**Zip:**__________
Country:____________**County:**__________
Phone 1:___________________**Ext:** ______
Phone 2:___________________**Ext:** ______
Fax 1:______________________________
Fax 2:______________________________
Email:______________________________
URL:_______________________________
User Name:________________**CS:** _______
User ID: ______________**Reminder:**__________
Password:_________**Confirm #:**_____**CS:**____
Search Word:__________________________
Listed On:___________________________
Catagory:___________________________
Product:____________________________
Also See:____________________________
Notes:______________________________
____
_______________________________________.

NOTES:
____
____
____
____
____
____
____
____
____
____
____
____.

WEB SITE LOG ____

NOTES

Web Site Name:________________________
Company Name:________________________
Contact Person 1:______________________
Contact Person 2:______________________
Purchase Order #:________**Invoice #:**_______
Date:___________________
Title 1:________________**Dept:**__________
Title 2:________________**Dept:**__________
Address:______________________________
City:_________________________________
State:___________________**Zip:**__________
Country:____________**County:**__________
Phone 1:___________________**Ext:** ______
Phone 2:___________________**Ext:** ______
Fax 1:_______________________________
Fax 2:_______________________________
Email:_______________________________
URL:________________________________
User Name:_______________**CS:** _______
User ID: _______________**Reminder:**_________
Password:_________**Confirm #:**_____**CS:**____
Search Word:___________________________
Listed On:____________________________
Catagory:____________________________
Product:_____________________________
Also See:____________________________
Notes:______________________________
____
_______________________________________.

NOTES:

____
____
____
____
____
____
____
____
____
____
____
____.

WEB SITE LOG ____

NOTES

Web Site Name:___________________________
Company Name:___________________________
Contact Person 1:________________________
Contact Person 2:________________________
Purchase Order #:_________**Invoice #:**_______
Date:____________________
Title 1:_________________**Dept:**___________
Title 2:_________________**Dept:**___________
Address:_________________________________
City:____________________________________
State:__________________**Zip:**___________
Country:_____________**County:**___________
Phone 1:_____________________**Ext:** ______
Phone 2:_____________________**Ext:** ______
Fax 1:___________________________________
Fax 2:___________________________________
Email:___________________________________
URL:____________________________________
User Name:_________________**CS:** _______
User ID: ______________**Reminder:**_________
Password:__________**Confirm #:**_____**CS:**____
Search Word:_____________________________
Listed On:_______________________________
Catagory:_______________________________
Product:________________________________
Also See:________________________________
Notes:__________________________________
____
____.

NOTES:

____
____
____
____
____
____
____
____
____
____
____
____.

WEB SITE LOG ____

NOTES

Web Site Name:________________________
Company Name:________________________
Contact Person 1:______________________
Contact Person 2:______________________
Purchase Order #:________**Invoice #:**_______
Date:__________________
Title 1:_______________**Dept:**__________
Title 2:_______________**Dept:**__________
Address:______________________________
City:_________________________________
State:________________**Zip:**__________
Country:____________**County:**__________
Phone 1:___________________**Ext:** ______
Phone 2:___________________**Ext:** ______
Fax 1:_______________________________
Fax 2:_______________________________
Email:_______________________________
URL:________________________________
User Name:_______________**CS**: _______
User ID: _____________**Reminder:**_________
Password:__________**Confirm #:**_____**CS**:____
Search Word:___________________________
Listed On:____________________________
Catagory:_____________________________
Product:______________________________
Also See:_____________________________
Notes:_______________________________
____
____.

NOTES:
____
____
____
____
____
____
____
____
____
____
____
____.

WEB SITE LOG ____

NOTES

Web Site Name:________________________
Company Name:________________________
Contact Person 1:______________________
Contact Person 2:______________________
Purchase Order #:________**Invoice #:**_______
Date:__________________
Title 1:_______________**Dept:**__________
Title 2:_______________**Dept:**__________
Address:_____________________________
City:_______________________________
State:_________________**Zip:**__________
Country:____________**County:**__________
Phone 1:___________________**Ext:** ______
Phone 2:___________________**Ext:** ______
Fax 1:______________________________
Fax 2:______________________________
Email:______________________________
URL:_______________________________
User Name:________________**CS**: _______
User ID: ______________**Reminder:**_________
Password:_________**Confirm #:**_____**CS:**____
Search Word:__________________________
Listed On:___________________________
Catagory:___________________________
Product:____________________________
Also See:____________________________
Notes:______________________________
____
_______________________________________.

NOTES:

____
____
____
____
____
____
____
____
____
____
____
____.

WEB SITE LOG ____

NOTES

Web Site Name:____________________________
Company Name:____________________________
Contact Person 1:__________________________
Contact Person 2:__________________________
Purchase Order #:________**Invoice #:**_______
Date:____________________
Title 1:_______________**Dept:**__________
Title 2:_______________**Dept:**__________
Address:______________________________
City:________________________________
State:_________________**Zip:**__________
Country:____________**County:**__________
Phone 1:___________________**Ext:** ______
Phone 2:___________________**Ext:** ______
Fax 1:_______________________________
Fax 2:_______________________________
Email:_______________________________
URL:________________________________
User Name:________________**CS:** _______
User ID: ______________**Reminder:**_________
Password:_________**Confirm #:**_____**CS:**____
Search Word:____________________________
Listed On:_____________________________
Catagory:______________________________
Product:______________________________
Also See:_____________________________
Notes:________________________________
____
____.

NOTES:

____
____
____
____
____
____
____
____
____
____
____
____.

WEB SITE LOG ____

NOTES

Web Site Name:________________________
Company Name:________________________
Contact Person 1:_____________________
Contact Person 2:_____________________
Purchase Order #:________**Invoice #:**______
Date:__________________
Title 1:______________**Dept:**__________
Title 2:______________**Dept:**__________
Address:______________________________
City:_________________________________
State:_________________**Zip:**__________
Country:____________**County:**__________
Phone 1:___________________**Ext:** _____
Phone 2:___________________**Ext:** _____
Fax 1:________________________________
Fax 2:________________________________
Email:________________________________
URL:_________________________________
User Name:________________**CS:** ______
User ID: ______________**Reminder:**________
Password:_________**Confirm #:**_____**CS:**____
Search Word:___________________________
Listed On:_____________________________
Catagory:_____________________________
Product:______________________________
Also See:_____________________________
Notes:________________________________
____
____.

NOTES:

____
____
____
____
____
____
____
____
____
____
____
____.

WEB SITE LOG ____

NOTES

Web Site Name:______________________
Company Name:______________________
Contact Person 1:____________________
Contact Person 2:____________________
Purchase Order #:________**Invoice #:**______
Date:__________________
Title 1:______________**Dept:**__________
Title 2:______________**Dept:**__________
Address:____________________________
City:______________________________
State:_______________**Zip:**__________
Country:___________**County:**__________
Phone 1:_________________**Ext:** _____
Phone 2:_________________**Ext:** _____
Fax 1:_____________________________
Fax 2:_____________________________
Email:_____________________________
URL:______________________________
User Name:______________**CS:** ______
User ID: ____________**Reminder:**________
Password:_________**Confirm #:**_____**CS:**____
Search Word:_________________________
Listed On:__________________________
Catagory:___________________________
Product:___________________________
Also See:___________________________
Notes:_____________________________
____
_____________________________________.

NOTES:

____
____
____
____
____
____
____
____
____
____
____
____.

WEB SITE LOG ____

NOTES

Web Site Name:___________________________
Company Name:___________________________
Contact Person 1:________________________
Contact Person 2:________________________
Purchase Order #:_________**Invoice #:**_______
Date:____________________
Title 1:________________**Dept:**___________
Title 2:________________**Dept:**___________
Address:_______________________________
City:__________________________________
State:__________________**Zip:**___________
Country:_____________**County:**___________
Phone 1:_____________________**Ext:** ______
Phone 2:_____________________**Ext:** ______
Fax 1:_________________________________
Fax 2:_________________________________
Email:_________________________________
URL:__________________________________
User Name:________________**CS:** _______
User ID: ______________**Reminder:**_________
Password:__________**Confirm #:**_____**CS:**____
Search Word:____________________________
Listed On:_____________________________
Catagory:______________________________
Product:_______________________________
Also See:_______________________________
Notes:_________________________________
____
____.

NOTES:

____
____
____
____
____
____
____
____
____
____
____
____.

WEB SITE LOG ____

NOTES

Web Site Name:________________________
Company Name:________________________
Contact Person 1:______________________
Contact Person 2:______________________
Purchase Order #:________**Invoice #:**_______
Date:___________________
Title 1:______________**Dept:**__________
Title 2:______________**Dept:**__________
Address:____________________________
City:_______________________________
State:________________**Zip:**__________
Country:____________**County:**__________
Phone 1:___________________**Ext:** ______
Phone 2:___________________**Ext:** ______
Fax 1:______________________________
Fax 2:______________________________
Email:______________________________
URL:_______________________________
User Name:_______________**CS:** _______
User ID: _____________**Reminder:**_________
Password:_________**Confirm #:**_____**CS:**____
Search Word:__________________________
Listed On:___________________________
Catagory:____________________________
Product:____________________________
Also See:____________________________
Notes:______________________________
____
_______________________________________.

NOTES:

____
____
____
____
____
____
____
____
____
____
____
____.

WEB SITE LOG ____

NOTES

Web Site Name:___________________________
Company Name:___________________________
Contact Person 1:________________________
Contact Person 2:________________________
Purchase Order #:_________**Invoice #:**_______
Date:____________________
Title 1:________________**Dept:**___________
Title 2:________________**Dept:**___________
Address:________________________________
City:___________________________________
State:__________________**Zip:**___________
Country:_____________**County:**___________
Phone 1:_____________________**Ext:** ______
Phone 2:_____________________**Ext:** ______
Fax 1:__________________________________
Fax 2:__________________________________
Email:__________________________________
URL:___________________________________
User Name:_________________**CS:** _______
User ID: ______________**Reminder:**_________
Password:__________**Confirm #:**_____**CS:**____
Search Word:_____________________________
Listed On:_______________________________
Catagory:_______________________________
Product:________________________________
Also See:_______________________________
Notes:_________________________________
____
____.

NOTES:

____
____
____
____
____
____
____
____
____
____
____
____.

WEB SITE LOG _____

NOTES

Web Site Name:___________________________
Company Name:___________________________
Contact Person 1:_________________________
Contact Person 2:_________________________
Purchase Order #:_________**Invoice #:**_______
Date:____________________
Title 1:_________________**Dept:**___________
Title 2:_________________**Dept:**___________
Address:________________________________
City:___________________________________
State:__________________**Zip:**___________
Country:_____________**County:**___________
Phone 1:____________________**Ext:** ______
Phone 2:____________________**Ext:** ______
Fax 1:__________________________________
Fax 2:__________________________________
Email:__________________________________
URL:___________________________________
User Name:_________________**CS**: _______
User ID: ______________**Reminder:**_________
Password:__________**Confirm #:**_____**CS**:____
Search Word:______________________________
Listed On:_______________________________
Catagory:_______________________________
Product:________________________________
Also See:_______________________________
Notes:_________________________________
____
____.

NOTES:
____
____
____
____
____
____
____
____
____
____
____
____.

WEB SITE LOG ____

NOTES

Web Site Name:__________________________
Company Name:__________________________
Contact Person 1:______________________
Contact Person 2:______________________
Purchase Order #:________**Invoice #:**_______
Date:____________________
Title 1:________________**Dept:**__________
Title 2:________________**Dept:**__________
Address:________________________________
City:___________________________________
State:__________________**Zip:**__________
Country:_____________**County:**__________
Phone 1:____________________**Ext:** ______
Phone 2:____________________**Ext:** ______
Fax 1:__________________________________
Fax 2:__________________________________
Email:__________________________________
URL:____________________________________
User Name:________________**CS:** _______
User ID: ______________**Reminder:**_________
Password:__________**Confirm #:**_____**CS:**____
Search Word:____________________________
Listed On:______________________________
Catagory:_______________________________
Product:________________________________
Also See:_______________________________
Notes:__________________________________
____
____.

NOTES:

____
____
____
____
____
____
____
____
____
____
____
____.

WEB SITE LOG ____

NOTES

Web Site Name:______________________
Company Name:______________________
Contact Person 1:____________________
Contact Person 2:____________________
Purchase Order #:_________**Invoice #:**_______
Date:_________________
Title 1:_______________**Dept:**_________
Title 2:_______________**Dept:**_________
Address:___________________________
City:______________________________
State:________________**Zip:**_________
Country:____________**County:**_________
Phone 1:__________________**Ext:** _____
Phone 2:__________________**Ext:** _____
Fax 1:____________________________
Fax 2:____________________________
Email:____________________________
URL:_____________________________
User Name:______________**CS:** ______
User ID: ______________**Reminder:**________
Password:_________**Confirm #:**_____**CS:**____
Search Word:________________________
Listed On:__________________________
Catagory:__________________________
Product:___________________________
Also See:__________________________
Notes:____________________________
____
_____________________________________.

NOTES:
____
____
____
____
____
____
____
____
____
____
____
____.

WEB SITE LOG ____

NOTES

Web Site Name:__________________________
Company Name:__________________________
Contact Person 1:_______________________
Contact Person 2:_______________________
Purchase Order #:_________**Invoice #:**_______
Date:____________________
Title 1:________________**Dept:**___________
Title 2:________________**Dept:**___________
Address:________________________________
City:___________________________________
State:__________________**Zip:**___________
Country:_____________**County:**___________
Phone 1:____________________**Ext:** ______
Phone 2:____________________**Ext:** ______
Fax 1:__________________________________
Fax 2:__________________________________
Email:__________________________________
URL:____________________________________
User Name:_________________**CS:** _______
User ID: ______________**Reminder:**_________
Password:__________**Confirm #:**_____**CS:**____
Search Word:____________________________
Listed On:______________________________
Catagory:_______________________________
Product:________________________________
Also See:_______________________________
Notes:__________________________________
____
____.

NOTES:

____
____
____
____
____
____
____
____
____
____
____
____.

WEB SITE LOG ____

NOTES

Web Site Name:___________________________
Company Name:___________________________
Contact Person 1:________________________
Contact Person 2:________________________
Purchase Order #:_________**Invoice #:**_______
Date:____________________
Title 1:________________**Dept:**___________
Title 2:________________**Dept:**___________
Address:________________________________
City:___________________________________
State:___________________**Zip:**___________
Country:_____________**County:**___________
Phone 1:_____________________**Ext:** ______
Phone 2:_____________________**Ext:** ______
Fax 1:__________________________________
Fax 2:__________________________________
Email:__________________________________
URL:___________________________________
User Name:_________________**CS:** _______
User ID: ______________**Reminder:**_________
Password:__________**Confirm #:**_____**CS:**____
Search Word:____________________________
Listed On:______________________________
Catagory:______________________________
Product:_______________________________
Also See:______________________________
Notes:_________________________________
____
____.

NOTES:

____
____
____
____
____
____
____
____
____
____
____
____.

INSTRUCTIONS FOR USING THE SOFTWARE LOG

The day will come you will need to reinstall your software using long ID numbers you can't possibly memorize. If these numbers are lost, stolen or destroyed, installation can not continue, but by logging the information, you will be up and running in no time at all. Software installation is easy; however, many programs simply will not install properly or in a configuration you want them to using the software manufacturers recommended installation. Sound familiar? The installation menus choices can be troublesome.

You may need to use custom install and select or deselect certain items. You'll never remember all of these troublesome quirks, so the computer will steal more of your time and build your frustration. Use the Software Log and your troubles are over!

EXAMPLE - SOFTWARE LOG__A__

NOTES

Program: Hewlett Packard Printer Driver
Registration #: A01-42-77633-PBaxt2 **CS:** Yes
Serial #: B2N5-09T4 **CS:** No
Key #: ZX7ubt8-917 **CS:** Yes
Other #: Reorder # 25905
Purchased from: Micro Software $5, 9-3-2010
Company Info on Page: # 4 and 21
Page number refer to this address book.
File: hp4drv.exe
Version: 14.2a **Date:** September 3, 2010
Patches: 15.2b installed on November 4, 2011
Comments: Patch failed, deleted from drive. Patch 16.1a worked fine, cured font errors.
Purpose: Serves HP-4 Laser Jet in Sales Dept.
Backup: Located on Zip Drive #4 in Safe Deposit
Install: Shut off anti-virus software first, as it conflicted and refused to install. Have Windows disk ready, it is needed during installation. Select "no" when asked if file should be placed in Windows directory. Reboot with Windows disk inserted or program will not install.
Settings: Go to Start, Printers, click on HP and change settings to 8x11size paper, 600 dpi, envelopes upper tray, uncheck raster setting.
Crashes: Print Overrun locks up printer using graphics program. Print only 20 pages at a time.
Notes: If printer won't work, reinstall driver software with printer on, reboot computer and reset printer using printer's touch pad button.

NOTES:
____
____
____
____.

SOFTWARE LOG ____

NOTES

Program: ______________________
Registration #: ____________ **CS:** ____
Serial #: ________________ **CS:** ____
Key #: ________________ **CS:** ____
Other #: ______________________
Purchased from: ________________
Company Info on Page #: ____________
Page number refer to this address book.
File: ______________________
Version: ________ **Date:** ____________
Patches: ______________________
Comments: ______________________
______________________.
Purpose: ______________________
Backup: ______________________
Install: ______________________
____
____
____
______________________.
Settings: ______________________
____
______________________.
Crashes: ______________________
______________________.
Notes: ______________________
____
______________________.

NOTES:
____
____
____.

SOFTWARE LOG ____

NOTES

Program: ______________________________
Registration #: __________________**CS:** ____
Serial #: ________________________**CS:**____
Key #: ________________________ **CS:**____
Other #: _______________________________
Purchased from: ______________________
Company Info on Page #:________________
Page number refer to this address book.
File: ___________________________________
Version: ________ **Date:** ______________
Patches: ______________________________
Comments: ____________________________
_______________________________________.
Purpose: ______________________________
Backup: ______________________________
Install: _______________________________
____
____
____
_______________________________________.
Settings: ______________________________
____
_______________________________________.
Crashes: ______________________________
_______________________________________.
Notes: ________________________________
____
_______________________________________.

NOTES:

____
____
____
____
____
____
____
____
____
____
____
____
____
____
____
____
____
____
____
____
____.

SOFTWARE LOG ____

NOTES

Program: ______________________________
Registration #: __________________**CS:** ____
Serial #: ______________________**CS:**____
Key #: _______________________ **CS:**____
Other #: ______________________________
Purchased from: ______________________
Company Info on Page #:________________
Page number refer to this address book.
File: _________________________________
Version: ________ **Date:** ______________
Patches: ______________________________
Comments: ___________________________
______________________________________.
Purpose: ______________________________
Backup: ______________________________
Install: _______________________________
____
____
____
______________________________________.
Settings: ______________________________
____
______________________________________.
Crashes: ______________________________
______________________________________.
Notes: ________________________________
____
______________________________________.

NOTES:

SOFTWARE LOG ____

NOTES

Program: ______________________________
Registration #: ________________**CS:** ___
Serial #: _______________________**CS:**___
Key #: _________________________ **CS:**___
Other #: ______________________________
Purchased from: _______________________
Company Info on Page #:________________
Page number refer to this address book.
File: _________________________________
Version: ________ **Date:** ______________
Patches: ______________________________
Comments: ____________________________
_______________________________________.
Purpose: ______________________________
Backup: ______________________________
Install: _______________________________
____
____
____
_______________________________________.
Settings: ______________________________
____
_______________________________________.
Crashes: ______________________________
_______________________________________.
Notes: ________________________________
____
_______________________________________.

NOTES:

SOFTWARE LOG ____

NOTES

Program: ______________________________
Registration #: ___________________**CS:** ____
Serial #: ________________________**CS:**____
Key #: __________________________ **CS:**_____
Other #: ________________________________
Purchased from: ______________________
Company Info on Page #:________________
Page number refer to this address book.
File: ________________________________
Version: ________ **Date:** ______________
Patches: ______________________________
Comments: ____________________________
____.
Purpose: ______________________________
Backup: ______________________________
Install: ______________________________
____
____
____
____.
Settings: _____________________________
____
____.
Crashes: _____________________________
____.
Notes: _______________________________
____
____.

NOTES:

SOFTWARE LOG ____

NOTES

Program: ______________________________
Registration #: __________________**CS:** ____
Serial #: _______________________**CS:**____
Key #: _______________________ **CS:**____
Other #: ______________________________
Purchased from: ______________________
Company Info on Page #:_______________
Page number refer to this address book.
File: _________________________________
Version: ________ **Date:** ______________
Patches: ______________________________
Comments: ____________________________
_______________________________________.
Purpose: ______________________________
Backup: ______________________________
Install: _______________________________
____
____
____
_______________________________________.
Settings: ______________________________
____
_______________________________________.
Crashes: ______________________________
_______________________________________.
Notes: ________________________________
____
_______________________________________.

NOTES:

SOFTWARE LOG ____

NOTES

Program: ________________________________
Registration #: __________________**CS:** ____
Serial #: ________________________**CS:**____
Key #: _________________________ **CS:**____
Other #: _________________________________
Purchased from: ______________________
Company Info on Page #:__________________
Page number refer to this address book.
File: ___________________________________
Version: _________ **Date:** _______________
Patches: _________________________________
Comments: ______________________________
____.
Purpose: ________________________________
Backup: _________________________________
Install: _________________________________
____
____
____
____.
Settings: ________________________________
____
____.
Crashes: ________________________________
____.
Notes: __________________________________
____
____.

NOTES:

SOFTWARE LOG ____

NOTES

Program: ________________________________
Registration #: ____________________**CS:** ____
Serial #: ________________________**CS:**____
Key #: ________________________ **CS:**____
Other #: ________________________________
Purchased from: ______________________
Company Info on Page #:_________________
Page number refer to this address book.
File: ________________________________
Version: ________ **Date:** ______________
Patches: ______________________________
Comments: ____________________________
____.
Purpose: _______________________________
Backup: _______________________________
Install: ________________________________
____
____
____
____.
Settings: _______________________________
____
____.
Crashes: _______________________________
____.
Notes: _________________________________
____
____.

NOTES:

SOFTWARE LOG ____

NOTES

Program: ______________________________
Registration #: __________________**CS:** ____
Serial #: _______________________**CS:**____
Key #: ________________________ **CS:**____
Other #: ________________________________
Purchased from: _________________________
Company Info on Page #:________________
Page number refer to this address book.
File: _________________________________
Version: ________ **Date:** ______________
Patches: _____________________________
Comments: ____________________________
____.
Purpose: ______________________________
Backup: ______________________________
Install: ________________________________
____
____
____
____.
Settings: ______________________________
____
____.
Crashes: ______________________________
____.
Notes: ________________________________
____
____.

NOTES:

SOFTWARE LOG ____

NOTES

Program: ______________________________
Registration #: __________________**CS:** ____
Serial #: _______________________**CS:**___
Key #: ________________________ **CS:**___
Other #: ______________________________
Purchased from: ______________________
Company Info on Page #:________________
Page number refer to this address book.
File: _________________________________
Version: ________ **Date:** ______________
Patches: ______________________________
Comments: ____________________________
______________________________________.
Purpose: ______________________________
Backup: ______________________________
Install: _______________________________
____
____
____
______________________________________.
Settings: ______________________________
____
______________________________________.
Crashes: ______________________________
______________________________________.
Notes: ________________________________
____
______________________________________.

NOTES:
____
____
____
____
____
____
____
____
____
____
____
____
____
____
____
____
____
____
____
____
____.

SOFTWARE LOG ____

NOTES

Program: ______________________________
Registration #: ________________ **CS:** ____
Serial #: ______________________ **CS:** ____
Key #: ________________________ **CS:** ____
Other #: ______________________________
Purchased from: ______________________
Company Info on Page #: ________________
Page number refer to this address book.
File: ________________________________
Version: ________ **Date:** ______________
Patches: ______________________________
Comments: ____________________________
_______________________________________.
Purpose: ______________________________
Backup: ______________________________
Install: _______________________________
____
____
____
_______________________________________.
Settings: ______________________________
____
_______________________________________.
Crashes: ______________________________
_______________________________________.
Notes: _________________________________
____
_______________________________________.

NOTES:

SOFTWARE LOG ____

NOTES

Program: ________________________________
Registration #: ___________________ **CS:** ____
Serial #: _______________________ **CS:**____
Key #: _________________________ **CS:**____
Other #: _________________________________
Purchased from: _______________________
Company Info on Page #:________________
Page number refer to this address book.
File: ___________________________________
Version: ________ **Date:** ______________
Patches: _______________________________
Comments: _____________________________
____.
Purpose: _______________________________
Backup: _______________________________
Install: ________________________________
____
____
____
____.
Settings: ______________________________
____
____.
Crashes: ______________________________
____.
Notes: _________________________________
____
____.

NOTES:
____
____
____
____
____
____
____
____
____
____
____
____
____
____
____
____
____
____
____
____.

SOFTWARE LOG ____

NOTES

Program: ______________________________
Registration #: __________________ **CS:** ____
Serial #: _______________________ **CS:**____
Key #: ______________________ **CS:**____
Other #: ______________________________
Purchased from: __________________________
Company Info on Page #:__________________
Page number refer to this address book.
File: ______________________________
Version: ________ **Date:** ______________
Patches: ______________________________
Comments: ____________________________
______________________________________.
Purpose: ______________________________
Backup: ______________________________
Install: ______________________________
____
____
____
______________________________________.
Settings: ______________________________
____
______________________________________.
Crashes: ______________________________
______________________________________.
Notes: ________________________________
____
______________________________________.

NOTES:

SOFTWARE LOG ____

NOTES

Program: ______________________________
Registration #: __________________**CS:** ____
Serial #: ______________________**CS:**____
Key #: ________________________ **CS:**____
Other #: ______________________________
Purchased from: ______________________
Company Info on Page #:________________
Page number refer to this address book.
File: ________________________________
Version: ________ **Date:** ______________
Patches: ______________________________
Comments: ____________________________
______________________________________.
Purpose: ______________________________
Backup: ______________________________
Install: ______________________________
____
____
____
______________________________________.
Settings: ______________________________
____
______________________________________.
Crashes: ______________________________
______________________________________.
Notes: ________________________________
____
______________________________________.

NOTES:

____
____
____
____
____
____
____
____
____
____
____
____
____
____
____
____
____
____
____
____
____.

SOFTWARE LOG ____

NOTES

Program: ______________________________
Registration #: __________________**CS:** ___
Serial #: _______________________**CS:**___
Key #: _________________________ **CS:**___
Other #: ______________________________
Purchased from: ____________________
Company Info on Page #:______________
Page number refer to this address book.
File: ________________________________
Version: ________ **Date:** _____________
Patches: _____________________________
Comments: ___________________________
____.
Purpose: _____________________________
Backup: ______________________________
Install: _______________________________
____
____
____
____.
Settings: _____________________________
____
____.
Crashes: _____________________________
____.
Notes: ________________________________
____
____.

NOTES:

SOFTWARE LOG ____

NOTES

Program: ______________________________
Registration #: ________________**CS:** ____
Serial #: ______________________**CS:**____
Key #: ________________________ **CS:**____
Other #: ______________________________
Purchased from: ______________________
Company Info on Page #:________________
Page number refer to this address book.
File: _________________________________
Version: ________ **Date:** ______________
Patches: ______________________________
Comments: ____________________________
______________________________________.
Purpose: ______________________________
Backup: ______________________________
Install: ______________________________
____
____
____
______________________________________.
Settings: ______________________________
____
______________________________________.
Crashes: ______________________________
______________________________________.
Notes: ________________________________
____
______________________________________.

NOTES:

____
____
____
____
____
____
____
____
____
____
____
____
____
____
____
____
____
____
____
____
____.

SOFTWARE LOG _____

NOTES

Program: ______________________________
Registration #: __________________ **CS:** ____
Serial #: _______________________ **CS:** ____
Key #: _________________________ **CS:** ____
Other #: ______________________________
Purchased from: _______________________
Company Info on Page #: ________________
Page number refer to this address book.
File: _________________________________
Version: ________ **Date:** ______________
Patches: ______________________________
Comments: ____________________________
____.
Purpose: ______________________________
Backup: ______________________________
Install: _______________________________
____
____
____
____.
Settings: ______________________________
____
____.
Crashes: ______________________________
____.
Notes: ________________________________
____
____.

NOTES:

SOFTWARE LOG ____

NOTES

Program: ________________________________
Registration #: ___________________**CS:** ___
Serial #: ________________________**CS:**___
Key #: __________________________ **CS:**___
Other #: _________________________________
Purchased from: ___________________
Company Info on Page #:_______________
Page number refer to this address book.
File: ______________________________
Version: ________ **Date:** ___________
Patches: ____________________________
Comments: __________________________
____.
Purpose: ___________________________
Backup: ____________________________
Install: ____________________________
____
____
____
____.
Settings: ___________________________
____
____.
Crashes: ___________________________
____.
Notes: ______________________________
____
____.

NOTES:

____
____
____
____
____
____
____
____
____
____
____
____
____
____
____
____
____
____
____
____
____.

SOFTWARE LOG _____

NOTES

Program: ________________________________
Registration #: __________________CS: ____
Serial #: ________________________CS:____
Key #: ________________________ CS:____
Other #: ________________________________
Purchased from: ________________________
Company Info on Page #:_________________
Page number refer to this address book.
File: ________________________________
Version: ________ **Date:** ______________
Patches: ______________________________
Comments: ____________________________
____.
Purpose: _______________________________
Backup: _______________________________
Install: ________________________________
____
____
____
____.
Settings: ______________________________
____
____.
Crashes: ______________________________
____.
Notes: ________________________________
____
____.

NOTES:

SOFTWARE LOG ____

NOTES

Program: ________________________________
Registration #: __________________**CS:** ____
Serial #: ________________________**CS:**____
Key #: ________________________ **CS:**____
Other #: ________________________________
Purchased from: ______________________
Company Info on Page #:_________________
Page number refer to this address book.
File: ___________________________________
Version: _________ **Date:** ______________
Patches: ________________________________
Comments: ______________________________
____.
Purpose: ________________________________
Backup: ________________________________
Install: _________________________________
____
____
____
____.
Settings: ________________________________
____
____.
Crashes: ________________________________
____.
Notes: __________________________________
____
____.

NOTES:

SOFTWARE LOG ____

NOTES

Program: ________________________________
Registration #: __________________**CS:** ____
Serial #: ________________________**CS:**____
Key #: __________________________**CS:**____
Other #: ________________________________
Purchased from: ________________________
Company Info on Page #:________________
Page number refer to this address book.
File: ___________________________________
Version: _________ **Date:** ______________
Patches: ________________________________
Comments: ______________________________
____.
Purpose: ________________________________
Backup: ________________________________
Install: ________________________________
____
____
____
____.
Settings: ________________________________
____
____.
Crashes: ________________________________
____.
Notes: __________________________________
____
____.

NOTES:

SOFTWARE LOG ____

NOTES

Program: ________________________________
Registration #: ___________________**CS:** ____
Serial #: ________________________**CS:**____
Key #: __________________________ **CS:**____
Other #: _________________________________
Purchased from: ________________________
Company Info on Page #:________________
Page number refer to this address book.
File: ____________________________________
Version: _________ **Date:** ______________
Patches: _______________________________
Comments: ______________________________
____.
Purpose: ________________________________
Backup: ________________________________
Install: _________________________________
____
____
____
____.
Settings: _______________________________
____
____.
Crashes: _______________________________
____.
Notes: __________________________________
____
____.

NOTES:

SOFTWARE LOG ____

NOTES

Program: ______________________________
Registration #: __________________**CS:** ____
Serial #: ________________________**CS:**____
Key #: ________________________ **CS:**____
Other #: _______________________________
Purchased from: ______________________
Company Info on Page #:_________________
Page number refer to this address book.
File: ________________________________
Version: ________ **Date:** ______________
Patches: ______________________________
Comments: ____________________________
_______________________________________.
Purpose: ______________________________
Backup: ______________________________
Install: ______________________________
____
____
____
_______________________________________.
Settings: _____________________________
____
_______________________________________.
Crashes: _____________________________
_______________________________________.
Notes: _______________________________
____
_______________________________________.

NOTES:

INSTRUCTIONS FOR USING THE HARDWARE LOG

What is the letter "A" beside the Hardware Log heading for? You may have more than one computer, so "A" may be a home desktop Apple® brand, "D" may be a Dell® brand laptop, "M" may be your main Micron® brand business computer — you get the idea. Here you can log in the data for each computer device you own! Printer, external or internal computer devices, scanner or any peripheral or hardware device you own.

Don't forget to log in the hardware information in the *Device Settings Log*. Thankfully, with plug and play installation many device settings no longer need to be logged. There may be some settings or switches that must be thrown on the device. Use the *Device Settings Log* to record these settings. The kids, a cat, a dog or simply dusting the equipment can accidentally throw a switch or two and before you know it your computer's device will no longer function and you'll not know why!

EXAMPLE HARDWARE LOG - __A__

NOTES

Device: Hewlett Packard Printer
Street: Somewhere in Silicone Valley
City: Santa Clara
State: CA **Zip:** 95555 **Country:** USA
Phone 1 Customer Service: 1-800-222-4444
Phone 2 Tech Support: 1-800-222-5555
Phone 3 Other: Parts Orders: 1-800-222-2222
E-mail: hp@techsupport.com
Web Site: www.hpprint.com
Contact Person 1: John Doe
Contact Person 2: Jane Doe
Contact Person 3: Bill Doe
Model: Laser Jet 5a
Serial #: ABcaoTX1-00 **CS:** Yes
Parts List #: A27 on page 54 in user manual
Other #: Reorder # 25905
Company Info on Page #: 4
Page number above refer to this address book.
Version: 6.4 **Date:** September 3, 2015
Purpose: Serves HP-5a Laser Jet at reception ctr.
Settings: Irq motherboard had to be set to address 3A to work properly, Scuzi address 4, networked with Ethernet.
Notes: Printer is leased. See John Doe in computer dept for repairs and supplies at ext 772. Driver software updated on July 1, 2014. Lease expires on October 1, 2017. User manual in drawer 14. Error messages, shut off then restart.

NOTES:

____
____
____.

HARDWARE LOG _____

Device: __________________ **NOTES**
Street: __________________
City: ______________
State: __ **Zip:** ____ **Country:** __
Phone 1 Customer Service: ____________
Phone 2 Tech Support: ____________
Phone 3 Other: Parts Orders:__________
E-mail: __________________
Web Site: __________________
Contact Person 1: ____________
Contact Person 2: ____________
Contact Person 3: ____________
Model: __________________
Serial #: ________________ **CS:** ____
Parts List #: __________________
Other #: __________________
Company Info on Page #: __________
Page number above refer to this address book.
Version: ___ **Date:** ________________
Purpose: ________________________
Settings: ________________________

Notes: ________________________

NOTES:

HARDWARE LOG ____

NOTES

Device: ______________________
Street: ______________________
City: _______________
State: __ **Zip:** ____ **Country:** ___
Phone 1 Customer Service: _____________
Phone 2 Tech Support: _____________
Phone 3 Other: Parts Orders:___________
E-mail: ______________________
Web Site: ____________________
Contact Person 1: ______________
Contact Person 2: ______________
Contact Person 3: ______________
Model: __________________
Serial #: _________________ **CS:** _____
Parts List #: _________________________
Other #: _____________________
Company Info on Page #: ___________
Page number above refer to this address book.
Version: ____ **Date:** _________________
Purpose: ____________________________
Settings: ____________________________
____
____
Notes: _____________________________
____
____
____

NOTES:

____
____
____
____
____
____
____
____
____
____
____
____
____
____
____
____
____
____
____
____
____.

HARDWARE LOG ____

NOTES

Device: ________________________
Street: ________________________
City: _______________
State: __ **Zip:** _____ **Country:** ___
Phone 1 Customer Service: _____________
Phone 2 Tech Support: _____________
Phone 3 Other: Parts Orders:___________
E-mail: ______________________
Web Site: ____________________
Contact Person 1: ______________
Contact Person 2: ______________
Contact Person 3: ______________
Model: __________________
Serial #: __________________ **CS:** _____
Parts List #: _________________________
Other #: ______________________
Company Info on Page #: ___________
Page number above refer to this address book.
Version: ____ **Date:** _________________
Purpose: ______________________________
Settings: _____________________________
____
____
Notes: ______________________________
____
____
____

NOTES:

HARDWARE LOG ____

NOTES

Device: ________________________
Street: _________________________
City: ________________
State: __ **Zip:** _____ **Country:** ___
Phone 1 Customer Service: ______________
Phone 2 Tech Support: ______________
Phone 3 Other: Parts Orders:____________
E-mail: ________________________
Web Site: ______________________
Contact Person 1: _______________
Contact Person 2: _______________
Contact Person 3: _______________
Model: ____________________
Serial #: ___________________ **CS:** _____
Parts List #: __________________________
Other #: ______________________
Company Info on Page #: ____________
Page number above refer to this address book.
Version: ____ **Date:** ___________________
Purpose: ______________________________
Settings: ______________________________
____
____
Notes: _______________________________
____
____
____

NOTES:
____
____
____
____
____
____
____
____
____
____
____
____
____
____
____
____
____
____
____
____
____.

HARDWARE LOG ____

NOTES

Device: ________________________
Street: ________________________
City: ________________
State: __ **Zip:** _____ **Country:** ___
Phone 1 Customer Service: ______________
Phone 2 Tech Support: ______________
Phone 3 Other: Parts Orders:____________
E-mail: ________________________
Web Site: ______________________
Contact Person 1: _______________
Contact Person 2: _______________
Contact Person 3: _______________
Model: ____________________
Serial #: __________________ **CS:** _____
Parts List #: ______________________
Other #: ______________________
Company Info on Page #: ____________
Page number above refer to this address book.
Version: ____ **Date:** __________________
Purpose: ______________________________
Settings: ______________________________
____
____

Notes: ______________________________
____
____
____

NOTES:

HARDWARE LOG ____

NOTES

Device: ________________________
Street: ________________________
City: ______________
State: __ **Zip:** _____ **Country:** ___
Phone 1 Customer Service: ______________
Phone 2 Tech Support: ______________
Phone 3 Other: Parts Orders:____________
E-mail: ________________________
Web Site: ______________________
Contact Person 1: _______________
Contact Person 2: _______________
Contact Person 3: _______________
Model: ___________________
Serial #: ___________________ **CS:** _____
Parts List #: ___________________________
Other #: ______________________
Company Info on Page #: ____________
Page number above refer to this address book.
Version: ____ **Date:** ___________________
Purpose: ______________________________
Settings: ______________________________
____
____
Notes: _______________________________
____
____
____

NOTES:
____
____
____
____
____
____
____
____
____
____
____
____
____
____
____
____
____
____
____
____
____.

HARDWARE LOG ____

NOTES

Device: ______________________
Street: ______________________
City: ____________
State: __ **Zip:** ____ **Country:** ___
Phone 1 Customer Service: ____________
Phone 2 Tech Support: ____________
Phone 3 Other: Parts Orders: ___________
E-mail: ______________________
Web Site: ____________________
Contact Person 1: _____________
Contact Person 2: _____________
Contact Person 3: _____________
Model: __________________
Serial #: _________________ **CS:** _____
Parts List #: ______________________
Other #: ____________________
Company Info on Page #: __________
Page number above refer to this address book.
Version: ____ **Date:** ________________
Purpose: ___________________________
Settings: ___________________________
____
____
Notes: ____________________________
____
____
____

NOTES:
____
____
____
____
____
____
____
____
____
____
____
____
____
____
____
____
____
____
____
____
____.

HARDWARE LOG ____

NOTES

Device: ________________________
Street: _________________________
City: ________________
State: __ **Zip:** ____ **Country:** ___
Phone 1 Customer Service: ______________
Phone 2 Tech Support: ______________
Phone 3 Other: Parts Orders:____________
E-mail: ________________________
Web Site: _____________________
Contact Person 1: _______________
Contact Person 2: _______________
Contact Person 3: _______________
Model: ____________________
Serial #: ___________________ **CS:** _____
Parts List #: __________________________
Other #: ______________________
Company Info on Page #: ____________
Page number above refer to this address book.
Version: ____ **Date:** ___________________
Purpose: ______________________________
Settings: ______________________________
____
____
Notes: ________________________________
____
____
____

NOTES:

HARDWARE LOG ____

NOTES

Device: ________________________
Street: _________________________
City: ______________
State: __ **Zip:** _____ **Country:** ___
Phone 1 Customer Service: ______________
Phone 2 Tech Support: ______________
Phone 3 Other: Parts Orders:____________
E-mail: ________________________
Web Site: ______________________
Contact Person 1: ______________
Contact Person 2: ______________
Contact Person 3: ______________
Model: ___________________
Serial #: __________________ **CS:** _____
Parts List #: _________________________
Other #: ____________________
Company Info on Page #: ____________
Page number above refer to this address book.
Version: ____ **Date:** _________________
Purpose: _____________________________
Settings: _____________________________
____
____

Notes: _______________________________
____
____
____

NOTES:

INSTRUCTIONS FOR USING THE CMOS SETTINGS LOG

Some day your hard disk drive will fail and with it all of the data on your hard disk. Make sure you have a current backup of all the important data on your computer's hard drive. The CMOS contains the data your hard disk drive needs in order to function. To enter the CMOS refer to your computer owners manual. Usually, entering the CMOS area is as easy as pressing a key pad on your keyboard as the computer is starting. The CMOS screen data will appear. Copy what you see on the computer screen into the CMOS Setting Log. The letter "A" denotes the settings for your specific computer.

Your computer may require that you enter more data. We have inserted extra lines so you can write in the information unique to your computer. Don't worry about what the terms mean, just write them down as you see them. Make sure when you exit the CMOS area select the option where you can exit without making any changes to the CMOS.

Remember: if you fail to log in the CMOS data you will lose the setup data when your battery fails, virus attack or accidentally changing the setup files. Take fifteen minutes of your time now and save yourself repair costs and downtime. It's well worth the effort!

SAMPLE - CMOS SETTINGS LOG __A__

Computer: Micron, Inc. Desktop Home Office **NOTES**
Battery: CA1282 Duracell **Password:** BusyB4
Primary Master: C: ATA 66 Maxtor Fireball
Size: 2560 **Cyls:** 620 **Head:** 128 **Precomp:** 0
Land Z: 4959 **Sector:** 63 **Mode:** LBA
Secondary Slave: D: Quantum
Size: 3668 **Cyls:** 840 **Head:** 328 **Precomp:** 0
Land Z: 5560 **Sector:** 243 **Mode:** LBA
Memory: 640k **Ext:** 31744k **Other** 384k
Total Memory: 32768k **Type:** SDRam 333mhz
Other Settings:

NOTES:

CMOS SETTINGS LOG ____

Computer: ______________________ **NOTES**
Battery: ______________**Password:** ______
Primary Master: ______________
Size: ________ **Cyls:** ________**Head:** ________ **Precomp:** _____
Land Z: ______ **Sector:** _____**Mode:** _____
Secondary Slave: ____________
Size: ________ **Cyls:**________ **Head:** ________ **Precomp:** ________
Land Z:_________ **Sector:** ________ **Mode:** ________
Memory: _______ **Ext:** ________ **Other**
Total Memory: __________ **Type:** ____________________
Other Settings:
____
____
____
____
____
____
____
____
____
____
____
____.

NOTES:
____
____
____
____
____
____
____
____
____
____
____
____
____
____
____.

CMOS SETTINGS LOG ____

Computer: ___________________________ **NOTES**
Battery: ______________Password: _______
Primary Master: _______________________
Size: _______ Cyls: _______Head: _______ Precomp: _____
Land Z: _______ Sector: _____Mode: _____
Secondary Slave: ____________
Size: _______ Cyls:_______ Head: _______ Precomp: _______
Land Z:_________ Sector: _______ Mode: _______
Memory: _______ Ext: ________ Other _______
Total Memory: _________ Type: ____________________
Other Settings:

____
____
____
____
____
____
____
____
____
____
____
____.

NOTES:

____
____
____
____
____
____
____
____
____
____
____
____
____
____
____.

CMOS SETTINGS LOG ____

Computer: ____________________________ **NOTES**
Battery: ______________**Password:** ______
Primary Master: ____________________
Size: ________ **Cyls:** ________**Head:** ________ **Precomp:** _____
Land Z: _______ **Sector:** _____**Mode:** _____
Secondary Slave: ____________
Size: ________ **Cyls:**________ **Head:** ________ **Precomp:** ________
Land Z:_________ **Sector:** ________ **Mode:** ________
Memory: _______ **Ext:** ________ **Other** ________
Total Memory: __________ **Type:** ____________________
Other Settings:

____
____
____
____
____
____
____
____
____
____
____
__________________________________.

NOTES:

____
____
____
____
____
____
____
____
____
____
____
____
____
____
____.

CMOS SETTINGS LOG ____

NOTES

Computer: ___________________________
Battery: ______________**Password:** _______
Primary Master: _______________________
Size: ________ **Cyls:** ________**Head:** ________ **Precomp:** _____
Land Z: _______ **Sector:** _____**Mode:** _____
Secondary Slave: _____________
Size: ________ **Cyls:**________ **Head:** ________ **Precomp:** ________
Land Z:_________ **Sector:** ________ **Mode:** ________
Memory: _______ **Ext:** _________ **Other** ________
Total Memory: __________ **Type:** ____________________
Other Settings:

NOTES:

CMOS SETTINGS LOG ____

Computer: ____________________________ **NOTES**
Battery: ______________Password: _______
Primary Master: ________________________
Size: ________ Cyls: ________Head: ________ Precomp: _____
Land Z: _______ Sector: _____Mode: _____
Secondary Slave: _____________
Size: ________ Cyls:________ Head: ________ Precomp: ________
Land Z:_________ Sector: ________ Mode: ________
Memory: _______ Ext: _________ Other ________
Total Memory: __________ Type: _____________________
Other Settings:

____
____
____
____
____
____
____
____
____
____
____
____.

NOTES:

____
____
____
____
____
____
____
____
____
____
____
____
____
____
____.

CMOS SETTINGS LOG ____

Computer: ____________________________ **NOTES**
Battery: ______________Password: _______
Primary Master: ________________________
Size: ________ Cyls: ________Head: ________ Precomp: _____
Land Z: _______ Sector: _____Mode: _____
Secondary Slave: _____________
Size: ________ Cyls:________ Head: ________ Precomp: ________
Land Z:_________ Sector: ________ Mode: ________
Memory: _______ Ext: ________ Other ________
Total Memory: __________ Type: _____________________
Other Settings:

____
____
____
____
____
____
____
____
____
____
____
____.

NOTES:

____
____
____
____
____
____
____
____
____
____
____
____
____
____
____.

INSTRUCTIONS FOR USING THE BIOS SETTINGS LOG

The BIOS is an internal computer chip storing critical data settings. It is supplied power from an internal battery. When this battery fails you will lose your BIOS settings and the computer will not run or start automatically. It's a weak link inside your computer. Battery failure is not the only villain. A computer program virus may attack your BIOS settings, or one of the kids got into the BIOS and altered these critical settings.

In any case, logging the BIOS setting will save you a ton of headaches and spare you the expense and inconvenience of taking your computer in for repair. To enter the BIOS screen, follow the same instructions you used to enter the CMOS screen. Don't worry about what the terms mean, just write them down as you see them. Make sure when you exit the BIOS area select the option where you can exit without making any changes to the BIOS.

Remember: if you fail to log in the BIOS data you will lose the setup data when your battery fails, virus attack or accidentally changing the setup files. Take fifteen minutes of your time now and save yourself repair costs and downtime. It's well worth the effort!

SAMPLE BIOS SETUP SETTINGS LOG __A__

Bios: SAward 2A59FQIC **Version:** 2.3 **NOTES**
Virus: On **CPU Cache:** On
External Cache: On **Self-test:** On
Boot Sequence: A, C **Swap Floppy:** Off
Boot Floppy Seek: On **Numlock Status:** On
Gate A20 Option: Fast
Typmatic Rate: Off **Char/Sec** 6 **Delay** 250
Security: Setup **PCI/VGA Snoop:** Off
Assign IRQ for VGA: Off
OS Select Dram: Non-OS2
Shadow Ram C800-CBFFF **:** Off
Shadow Ram C600-CBFFF **:** On
Chipset Dram: 60ns **Precharge:** 3 **Lead:** 6/5
Burst: x222/x333 **Write:** x222 **ISA:** PCIclk/4
BiosCache: On **Video:** Off **Peer:** On
Features: Off **Parity:** On **Recovery:** 1
Memory Parity: Auto Hole: 15M-16M
Other Settings:

____
____
____
____
____
____
____
______________________________.

BIOS SETUP SETTING ____

Bios: ____________________ Version:_____ **NOTES**
Virus: ___ CPU Cache: ___________
External Cache: ____ Self-test: ________
Boot Sequence: _____ Swap Floppy: _____
Boot Floppy Seek: ____ Numlock Status: ____
Gate A20 Option: ________________
Typmatic Rate: ___ Char/Sec __ Delay:____
Security: ____ PCI/VGA Snoop: _________
Assign IRQ for VGA: _______
OS Select Dram: ____________
Shadow Ram _____________: __________
Shadow Ram _____________: __________
Chipset Dram: ___ Precharge: __ Lead:___
Burst:______ Write: _____ ISA: _______
BiosCache: ______ Video: ____ Peer: ___
Features: __ Parity: _____ Recovery: ___
Memory Parity: ____ Hole: ___
Other Settings:

NOTES:

BIOS SETUP SETTING _____

NOTES

Bios: ______________________ Version:______
Virus: ____ CPU Cache: _____________
External Cache: _____ Self-test: _________
Boot Sequence: ______ Swap Floppy: ______
Boot Floppy Seek: ____ Numlock Status: ____
Gate A20 Option: ___________________
Typmatic Rate: ____ Char/Sec __ Delay:____
Security: _____ PCI/VGA Snoop: __________
Assign IRQ for VGA: ________
OS Select Dram: ______________
Shadow Ram _______________: ___________
Shadow Ram _______________: ___________
Chipset Dram: ____ Precharge: __ Lead:____
Burst:_______ Write: _____ ISA: ________
BiosCache: _______ Video: _____ Peer: ____
Features: ___ Parity: ______ Recovery: ____
Memory Parity: ____ Hole: ____

Other Settings:

NOTES:

BIOS SETUP SETTING _____

NOTES

Bios: _____________________ Version:______
Virus: ____ CPU Cache: _____________
External Cache: _____ Self-test: _________
Boot Sequence: ______ Swap Floppy: ______
Boot Floppy Seek: ____ Numlock Status: ____
Gate A20 Option: ___________________
Typmatic Rate: ____ Char/Sec __ Delay:____
Security: _____ PCI/VGA Snoop: __________
Assign IRQ for VGA: ________
OS Select Dram: ______________
Shadow Ram _______________: ___________
Shadow Ram _______________: ___________
Chipset Dram: ____ Precharge: __ Lead:____
Burst:_______ Write: _____ ISA: ________
BiosCache: _______ Video: _____ Peer: ____
Features: ___ Parity: ______ Recovery: ____
Memory Parity: _____ Hole: ____
Other Settings:

____
____
____
____
____
____
____
____
____
____
____
____.

NOTES:

____
____
____
____
____
____
____
____
____
____
____
____
____
____
____.

BIOS SETUP SETTING ____

Bios: ____________________ Version:______ **NOTES**

Virus: ____ CPU Cache: ____________

External Cache: _____ Self-test: _________

Boot Sequence: ______ Swap Floppy: ______

Boot Floppy Seek: ____ Numlock Status: ____

Gate A20 Option: _________________

Typmatic Rate: ____ Char/Sec __ Delay:____

Security: _____ PCI/VGA Snoop: _________

Assign IRQ for VGA: _______

OS Select Dram: ____________

Shadow Ram ______________: __________

Shadow Ram ______________: __________

Chipset Dram: ____ Precharge: __ Lead:____

Burst:_______ Write: _____ ISA: _______

BiosCache: _______ Video: _____ Peer: ____

Features: ___ Parity: ______ Recovery: ____

Memory Parity: _____ Hole: ____

Other Settings:

NOTES:

BIOS SETUP SETTING ____

NOTES

Bios: ____________________ Version:_____
Virus: ____ CPU Cache: ____________
External Cache: _____ Self-test: _________
Boot Sequence: ______ Swap Floppy: ______
Boot Floppy Seek: ____ Numlock Status: ____
Gate A20 Option: _________________
Typmatic Rate: ____ Char/Sec __ Delay:____
Security: _____ PCI/VGA Snoop: _________
Assign IRQ for VGA: _______
OS Select Dram: _____________
Shadow Ram ______________: __________
Shadow Ram ______________: __________
Chipset Dram: ____ Precharge: __ Lead:____
Burst:_______ Write: _____ ISA: _______
BiosCache: _______ Video: _____ Peer: ____
Features: ___ Parity: ______ Recovery: ____
Memory Parity: _____ Hole: ____
Other Settings:

NOTES:

BIOS SETUP SETTING _____

Bios: ____________________ Version:______ **NOTES**
Virus: ____ CPU Cache: ____________
External Cache: _____ Self-test: _________
Boot Sequence: ______ Swap Floppy: ______
Boot Floppy Seek: ____ Numlock Status: ____
Gate A20 Option: _________________
Typmatic Rate: ____ Char/Sec __ Delay:____
Security: _____ PCI/VGA Snoop: _________
Assign IRQ for VGA: _______
OS Select Dram: ____________
Shadow Ram ______________: __________
Shadow Ram ______________: __________
Chipset Dram: ____ Precharge: __ Lead:____
Burst:_______ Write: _____ ISA: _______
BiosCache: _______ Video: _____ Peer: ____
Features: ___ Parity: _____ Recovery: ____
Memory Parity: _____ Hole: ____
Other Settings:

____
____
____
____
____
____
____
____
____
____
____
____.

NOTES:

____
____
____
____
____
____
____
____
____
____
____
____
____
____
____.

INSTRUCTIONS FOR USING THE DEVICE SETTINGS LOG

When any device is installed into a computer certain switches, jumper connections or other setting are usually made to the device. If you have a SCSI device installed you may need to set the ID to a specific number. Log the numbers and settings of all your devices.

The device setting supports four external hard drives and eight peripheral devices attached to one computer. More than most users will ever need!

SAMPLE - DEVICE SETTINGS __A__

COMPUTER: Micron Desktop at Office **NOTES**
External Drive 1: Zip® Drive
External Drive 2: Jaz 1-Gig® Drive
External Drive 3: On Stream®
External Drive 4: Jaz® 2-Gig Drive
External Drive 1 SCSI Address: 3
External Drive 2 SCSI Address: 4
External Drive 3 SCSI Address: 12
External Drive 4 SCSI Address: 8

Device 1 Scanner HP 6000®
Device 2 Printer Tektronics® Phaser 4
Device 3 Web Cam ABC Corp.®
Device 4 Fax Machine Zerox® Danka Omni Fax® MFP6000
Device 5 Drawing Tablet Technical Technics®
Device 6 Camera Nikon Pro®
Device 7 Bar Code Generator BarGraf®
Device 8 Label Printer Label Pro®

Device 1 SCSI Address: 5
Device 2 SCSI Address: 6
Device 3 SCSI Address: 7
Device41 SCSI Address: 9
Device 5 SCSI Address: 10
Device 6 SCSI Address: 11
Device 7 SCSI Address: 13
Device 8 SCSI Address: 14
Reserved SCSI Address: 1 and 2
Notes:________________________________
____
____
____

NOTES:
____
____
____
____
____.

DEVICE SETTINGS ____

<u>COMPUTER</u>: ______________ **<u>NOTES</u>**
External Drive 1: ______________
External Drive 2: ______________
External Drive 3: ______________
External Drive 4: ______________

External Drive 1 SCSI Address: _____
External Drive 2 SCSI Address: _____
External Drive 3 SCSI Address: _____
External Drive 4 SCSI Address: _____

Device 1 ____________________
Device 2 ____________________
Device 3 ____________________
Device 4 ____________________
Device 5 ____________________
Device 6 ____________________
Device 7 ____________________
Device 8 ____________________

Device 1 SCSI Address: _____
Device 2 SCSI Address: _____
Device 3 SCSI Address: _____
Device4 SCSI Address:_____
Device 5 SCSI Address: _____
Device 6 SCSI Address: _____
Device 7 SCSI Address: _____
Device 8 SCSI Address: _____
Reserved SCSI Address:_____
Notes:______________________________
____
____
____

NOTES:
____
____
____
____
____
____
____
____
____
____
____
____
____
____
____.

DEVICE SETTINGS ____

COMPUTER: __________________ **NOTES**

External Drive 1: _______________
External Drive 2: _______________
External Drive 3: _______________
External Drive 4: _______________

External Drive 1 SCSI Address: _____
External Drive 2 SCSI Address: _____
External Drive 3 SCSI Address: _____
External Drive 4 SCSI Address: _____

Device 1 _____________________
Device 2 _____________________
Device 3 _____________________
Device 4 _____________________
Device 5 _____________________
Device 6 _____________________
Device 7 _____________________
Device 8 _____________________

Device 1 SCSI Address: _____
Device 2 SCSI Address: _____
Device 3 SCSI Address: _____
Device4 SCSI Address:_____
Device 5 SCSI Address: _____
Device 6 SCSI Address: _____
Device 7 SCSI Address: _____
Device 8 SCSI Address: _____
Reserved SCSI Address:_____
Notes:________________________________
____
____
____

NOTES:

DEVICE SETTINGS ____

COMPUTER: ________________ **NOTES**

External Drive 1: ______________
External Drive 2: ______________
External Drive 3: ______________
External Drive 4: ______________

External Drive 1 SCSI Address: ____
External Drive 2 SCSI Address: ____
External Drive 3 SCSI Address: ____
External Drive 4 SCSI Address: ____

Device 1 ____________________
Device 2 ____________________
Device 3 ____________________
Device 4 ____________________
Device 5 ____________________
Device 6 ____________________
Device 7 ____________________
Device 8 ____________________

Device 1 SCSI Address: ____
Device 2 SCSI Address: ____
Device 3 SCSI Address: ____
Device4 SCSI Address:____
Device 5 SCSI Address: ____
Device 6 SCSI Address: ____
Device 7 SCSI Address: ____
Device 8 SCSI Address: ____
Reserved SCSI Address:____
Notes:______________________________
____
____
____

NOTES:

DEVICE SETTINGS ____

COMPUTER: ________________ **NOTES**

External Drive 1: ______________
External Drive 2: ______________
External Drive 3: ______________
External Drive 4: ______________

External Drive 1 SCSI Address: _____
External Drive 2 SCSI Address: _____
External Drive 3 SCSI Address: _____
External Drive 4 SCSI Address: _____

Device 1 ____________________
Device 2 ____________________
Device 3 ____________________
Device 4 ____________________
Device 5 ____________________
Device 6 ____________________
Device 7 ____________________
Device 8 ____________________

Device 1 SCSI Address: _____
Device 2 SCSI Address: _____
Device 3 SCSI Address: _____
Device4 SCSI Address:_____
Device 5 SCSI Address: _____
Device 6 SCSI Address: _____
Device 7 SCSI Address: _____
Device 8 SCSI Address: _____
Reserved SCSI Address:_____
Notes:______________________________
____
____
____

NOTES:
____
____
____
____
____
____
____
____
____
____
____
____
____
____
____.

DEVICE SETTINGS ____

COMPUTER: ________________ **NOTES**

External Drive 1: ____________

External Drive 2: ____________

External Drive 3: ____________

External Drive 4: ____________

External Drive 1 SCSI Address: ____

External Drive 2 SCSI Address: ____

External Drive 3 SCSI Address: ____

External Drive 4 SCSI Address: ____

Device 1 ________________

Device 2 ________________

Device 3 ________________

Device 4 ________________

Device 5 ________________

Device 6 ________________

Device 7 ________________

Device 8 ________________

Device 1 SCSI Address: ____

Device 2 SCSI Address: ____

Device 3 SCSI Address: ____

Device4 SCSI Address:____

Device 5 SCSI Address: ____

Device 6 SCSI Address: ____

Device 7 SCSI Address: ____

Device 8 SCSI Address: ____

Reserved SCSI Address:____

Notes:________________________

NOTES:

DEVICE SETTINGS ____

COMPUTER: __________________ **NOTES**

External Drive 1: _______________
External Drive 2: _______________
External Drive 3: _______________
External Drive 4: _______________

External Drive 1 SCSI Address: _____
External Drive 2 SCSI Address: _____
External Drive 3 SCSI Address: _____
External Drive 4 SCSI Address: _____

Device 1 _____________________
Device 2 _____________________
Device 3 _____________________
Device 4 _____________________
Device 5 _____________________
Device 6 _____________________
Device 7 _____________________
Device 8 _____________________

Device 1 SCSI Address: _____
Device 2 SCSI Address: _____
Device 3 SCSI Address: _____
Device4 SCSI Address:_____
Device 5 SCSI Address: _____
Device 6 SCSI Address: _____
Device 7 SCSI Address: _____
Device 8 SCSI Address: _____
Reserved SCSI Address:_____
Notes:_________________________________

NOTES:

THE 7 DAY PLAN TO BE A BETTER CHRISTIAN!

SUNDAY -- This is a day of rest (see Saturday) of which no work is to be performed. Take full advantage of it! However, extend extra kindness to others. Read the Word, listen to Christian radio and watch TV for faith comes by "hearing" the Word of God.

MONDAY -- Drive your vehicle with patience towards others. Be changed at work. No more gossip, complaining, bad jokes. Just start being nice -- Biblically correct! Be cooperative. Can you do this for just one day?

TUESDAY -- Forget Me! Do a good thing for another. Open doors, buy someone a meal or gift, feed a stranger's parking meter. Give so you will receive. Give something! The Lord gives, so should you.

WEDNESDAY -- Compliment Day! Say something nice to someone, including one who may not like you. Be sincere about it! If someone needs help, go to their aid. Make someone smile today!

THURSDAY -- Distribute a Bible track. No tracks? Make or buy some! It is time you begin your ministry to the Lord to share the Good News. There are many hurting people who need the Lord and it is your responsibility to introduce them to Him. Using tracks make the job easy!

FRIDAY -- Day of forgiveness! When you forgive others transgressions, you are released from the anguish within yourself. It is easy to do! Start the process today! See Tuesday and Wednesday's instructions. Life is so much easier to live and great mercy and blessing arrive when you forgive!

SATURDAY -- Rest if this is the Sabbath you honor or donate; time, items, food, or money to the homeless shelters. Do not forget the poor! Visit or call a relative or friend. Express your appreciation for what the Lord has given you! Share with others what you have and the Lord will give you even more!

Free Bible Tracks For SASE!

EACH DAY

Contact Us For Bible Tracks!

START the day right by greeting the Lord and giving thanks for all He has done and what He will do for you in the future. **END** the day right by expressing your gratitude to the Lord.

SPEAK often to the Lord, as he is your best friend. Remember, he wants to handle every detail in your life, even the small stuff. Do not become so busy in your day you leave Him out of your life.

WHEN you pray just speak as you would to a friend. There is no need for theatrical displays of emotions or insincerity. If you fall short, do not turn your face away from the Lord and hide. Take the issue to Him.

WHAT will you give to the Lord if He grants your request? Will you simply say thank you and forget Him until you need something else later? The Lord sees the suffering of the sick and poor. Why not pledge to help them? Make your promise and keep it! Do it now before you recieve. This is faith in action.

SPREAD the Word of God. You may not be a minister, but you can distribute tracks. Leave them everywhereyou go. Keep some on your person each day. Your reward shall be great! Write us for tracts!

TITHE to the Lord. Give and you shall recieve more! Give to churches, ministries, homeless shelters, or where there is dire need. A perfect expression of love for others! God's System Never Fails!

PRINT AND DISTRIBUTE TO OTHERS!

JAMES RUSSELL PUBLISHING

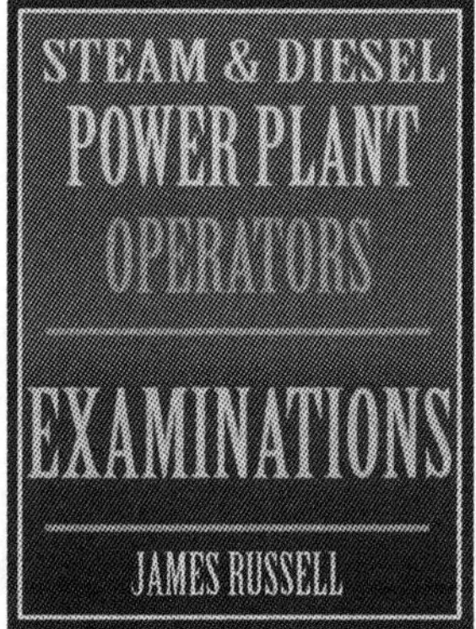

STEAM & DIESEL POWER PLANT OPERATORS EXAMINATIONS
ISBN 0-916367-088 117 pp., 8x11, illustrated, $34.95 Over 1,400 multiple-choice test questions & answers (with explanations) helps stationary engineer power plant operators pass steam boiler licensing and pre-employment exams. No other book compares with the sheer power to educate employees in the safe operation of plant equipment. A bestseller to the power plant industry since 1981. Questions from this book are used in city & state licensing and civil service exams!

TRAP SHOOTING SECRETS
ISBN 0-916367-096 183 pp., 8x11, 85 illustrations, $34.95. There has never been a book like this, ever! *TSS* is like having a shooting coach telling you precisely what to do to hit the targets. It is the first book ever to be endorsed by professional trap shooters! Hall of Fame and Olympic target shooters recommend this book! TSS transforms shooters into winning champions! All shotgun sports shooters benefit from these powerful instructions.

PRECISION SHOOTING - THE TRAPSHOOTER'S BIBLE
ISBN 0-916367-10X 117 pp., 8x11, 145 illustrations, $34.95. The *only* trap shooting book with ATA & Olympic Double-Trap technical instructions. The *only* professional advanced-level trapshooting book in the world. This target shooting book includes 315 questions & answers to master shooting proficiency. Readers obtain high-score results! Endorsed by professional shotgun shooting instructors. Winning advice for all shotgun sport shooters!

SCREEN & STAGE MARKETING SECRETS
ISBN 0-916367-118 177pp., 8x11, 60 illustrations, $34.95. This is the *only* book specifically written for writers to sell screenplays and stage plays to literary agents and the movie industry. Script formats, sample query letters, marketing instructions, contacting producers, stars, studios and even a valuable list of WGA agents willing to give readers of this book special consideration! No book compares with the marketing power of this book. Writer's learn how to sell their scripts!

ORDER YOUR BOOKS TODAY!

PUBLISHER DISCOUNTS
Bookstre Special Order 20%
Individuals $34.95
S & H $4 single copy.
E-mail:
screenplay@powernet.net

PUBLISHER - SAN 295-852X
James Russell Publishing
780 Diogenes Drive, Reno, NV 89512
Phone / Fax: (775)348-8711
www.powernet.net/~scrnplay

DISTRIBUTORS
Baker & Taylor (800)775-1100
www.btol.com
Ingrams (800)937-8000
www.ingrambook.com